EIGHTEEN
LESSONS
Wayne
FROM

Reflections on the Teachings of Dr. Wayne Dyer

ANN MARIE GANNESS

BALBOA.
PRESS
A DIVISION OF HAY HOUSE

Some names and identifying details have been changed
to protect the privacy of individuals.

Bible quotations taken from the New King James Version—
Broadman & Holman Publishers, Nashville, TN.

Balboa Press books may be ordered through booksellers or by contacting:

Balboa Press
A Division of Hay House
1663 Liberty Drive
Bloomington, IN 47403
www.balboapress.com
1 (877) 407-4847

Printed in the United States of America.

ISBN: 978-1-4525-8983-1 (sc)
ISBN: 978-1-4525-8985-5 (hc)
ISBN: 978-1-4525-8984-8 (e)

Library of Congress Control Number: 2014900248

Balboa Press rev. date: 1/21/2014

For my guardian angels, Andy Ganness
and Grandmother Rosie.

Contents

In the end, the answers always come from deep inside of us, from the very essence of who we are, our spirit … I call them "soul solutions."
—Ann Marie Ganness

Love and Freedom

May 3, 2013

It was close to 1:00 a.m. and my flight was about to touch down in Atlanta. I looked through the airplane window at the twinkling lights of the city and asked myself, "Are you really doing this, Ann Marie?" I felt empowered and optimistic but nervous. The spiritual and emotional shifts happening in my life left me breathless, and sometimes scared.

At the end of March 2013 I felt like my world was crumbling all around me; I felt deceived and betrayed by someone I truly cared for. The pain was so intense I couldn't even think clearly. I just knew that I had to keep praying. However, I am convinced that it was this pain that led me to Atlanta and to the "I Can Do It" Conference. My aunt introduced me to Dr. Wayne Dyer's teachings a few years ago when she gave me the book *Manifest Your Destiny*. After my divorce I became even more engrossed in what Dr. Dyer had to say, and this intensified as the months went by. I felt like he was the only author and speaker to whom I could relate. I developed an almost insatiable appetite for his philosophies and just really wanted to share his messages with others.

It was this desire to truly connect with my spirituality that led to me to Hay House Radio one afternoon in January 2013. Dr. Dyer's *Wishes Fulfilled* program was on, and I decided to try my luck at calling in.

My heart seemed to be racing as I dialed the number once … and then twice. As expected, I got a busy tone. The third time a voice welcomed me to Hay House Radio, I panicked, and I dropped the phone. I was so mad with myself! I tried again. Not surprisingly the line was busy. It was only after my fifth or sixth attempt at dialing that I got through. This time I was more in control, and I chatted amicably with the voice on the other end of the line for a couple of minutes. A few minutes later I was put through live to speak with Dr. Dyer. That conversation was a turning point in my life and helped me to embark on a journey of self-discovery that eventually led to me writing this book.

It also helped me to answer my own question, "What do you want your life to be, Ann Marie?" Oh, how I long for the peace that absolute spiritual connection brings. During my conversation with Dr. Dyer I asked him about his spiritual journey and what was next for him. Here's some of what he said:

> Rumi said when you are born, a ladder is placed before you to help you escape from this world, and I have always had this image of a ladder placed before me when I was born. I've been climbing that ladder, and I've been stepping one rung up. And as I've reviewed all of the things that have happened in my life and as I wrote *I Can See Clearly Now*, I can see how I was moving one step up from when I was a little boy, when I was in grade school, when I was in high school, when I was in service in the navy, when I was in college, when I was a professor, when I was writing.
>
> All of these decisions, the people who came into my life were helping me to step up one more rung on that

ladder. And I feel like what I have done is that I have gotten to that ladder to pretty much the top of how far it goes in the physical world. It's like there is a scaffold there, and I walk across that scaffold. The next step up for me is really just divine love of being in that place of just loving everything and everyone and having no judgment toward anyone.

I'm imagining myself on that ladder, just climbing one step at a time just like Dr. Dyer is doing, and this is what determines so many of the choices I now make. It is what encouraged to me to go to Atlanta and to eventually write this book.

My conversation that day ended with Dr. Dyer telling me that I should attend one of his conferences, but I had no idea at the time how to make that happen.

Fast-forward to four months later. I was actually checking into a hotel in Atlanta where the "I Can Do It" Conference was taking place. I knew in my heart that I was about to experience another profound and life-changing experience.

Before I left Trinidad, I was told by well-meaning friends that my chances of meeting Dr. Dyer were almost impossible. As I write, I'm looking at the photograph of us that was taken at the end of his talk, and it is indeed a reminder that we are all connected and are all part of one universal God energy. Of an audience of a couple thousand, for some inexplicable reason I was allowed on the stage, where I got the chance to say, "Thank you, Dr. Dyer, for saving me."

There are several other objects on my desk, and I draw on their energy as I write. There is a ceramic plaque that was given to me by my aunt about twenty-five years ago, with the inscription, "Lord, help me to remember that nothing is going to happen to me today that you and I together can't handle." There is also an angel made out of straw given to me by a friend who brought it back from a visit to the Philippines. There is a candle with an image of the Virgin Mary on it and a photo of me with a scarf around my head. I've also kept my name tag from the conference, which says, "I Can Do It, Atlanta—Ann Marie Ganness." While this may seem insignificant, these simple words, "I can do it," kept me going during the months I was writing. I also have in front of me four of Dr. Dyer's books—*Manifest Your Destiny, Wishes Fulfilled, The Power of Intention*, and *Change Your Thoughts, Change Your Life*.

I smile to myself when I think about the sequence of events that led to me writing *Eighteen Lessons*. They are truly intriguing but not surprising since now I understand there really are no coincidences. When I started writing, I had no idea what the title would be or what the format would look like. I just knew that I had to write a book. One day the answer came to me. "Use the lessons you have learned from Dr. Dyer to give people hope."

People ask me all the time about the connection I feel to Dr. Dyer's philosophies. I've recognized that a large part of that appeal has to do with me truly appreciating his humanness.

So why have I used the number eighteen in this book title? Well, I read that *one* in numerology represents new beginnings and creation, and that it is also associated with the sun. The sun is said to represent life and the divine spark at the center of the universe. The number *eight* represents infinity. Together that makes eighteen, a number that seems to be suggesting "the beginning of infinity."

The chapters in *Eighteen Lessons from Wayne* are based on my personal experiences and insights as I continue on my path of discovering true self-reliance. Like so many of you reading this book, I have many unanswered questions, and yes, I do experience moments of doubt and insecurity. However, I have begun to embrace these and think of them as passing clouds along my journey. After all, they are part of the process. I have a vision and a mission, and I am on a treasure hunt for the things in life that cannot be defined but are felt deep within. As Dr. Dyer said during my conversation with him on Hay House Radio, "Freedom comes when you can just be an instrument of love."

LESSON 1

We Are All Connected

As I continue along this journey, I have asked myself repeatedly, "Is this what I have been called to do?" The answer is always yes. Despite the insecurities about whether my insights will resonate with others, I truly believe that my purpose is to spread messages of hope. It is with this knowing deep within that I have chosen to go in my current direction.

I know and fully accept that absolutely nothing happens by accident. It is as a result of our own manifestation, consciously or unconsciously. People say that nothing happens before its time, and the lesson of "I am that I am" was delivered to me at the time it was supposed to.

May 13, 2013, was the night I saw the movie *The Moses Code* for the first time. While I was watching it, I felt the hair at the back of my neck stand on end. For the past few months I had been embracing wholeheartedly the concept of everyone being connected, of us being part of God and vice versa. *The Moses Code* attempts to explain the concept of "I am that I am." According to the Bible, those words were told to Moses by God when Moses questioned God about his ability to lead the Israelites to "a land flowing with milk and honey." Exodus 3:13–15 (NKJV) says,

And Moses said to God, Behold, when I come to the children of Israel, and shall say to them, The God of your fathers has sent me to you; and they shall say to me, what is his name? what shall I say to them? And God said to Moses, I AM THAT I AM: and he said, Thus shall you say to the children of Israel, I AM has sent me to you. And God said moreover to Moses, Thus shall you say to the children of Israel, the LORD God of your fathers, the God of Abraham, the God of Isaac, and the God of Jacob, has sent me to you: this is my name for ever, and this is my memorial to all generations.

I first became aware of the existence of *The Moses Code* through the teachings of Dr. Dyer. I was introduced to *I Am Meditations*, a CD that he did with James Twyman. I was looking at a video of one of his talks when he gave away the CD, and I thought to myself, *Oh, I want that.* I also went onto YouTube and was able to find some of the meditations. Since then I had been doing the meditations, and every time I listen to them, I feel the power of God moving within me. I imagine the scene when Moses stood in front of that burning bush and God said to him, "I am that I am," and he said, "Thus, you shall say to the children of Israel, 'I am has sent me to you.'" I have also come across those words, "I am," repeatedly while I have read the Bible in recent months. Then one day I discovered the film *The Moses Code* on YouTube. How it happened really does give validity to the concept that when we focus on something, it will make itself visible in our lives.

The morning of the day I saw the film for the first time was a challenging one for me. My mother had to visit her doctor to get the results of some blood tests she had done a few days before. She was scared, and my father and I were worried. I wasn't able to go with her to the appointment since I had a work deadline I had to meet. She wasn't looking her best, which added to my concern. On the morning of the doctor's visit I awoke and immediately said a silent prayer while I was still in bed. She and my father left for the doctor's appointment, and I tried not to worry too much. Instead I called on God to watch over both my parents and to just "make everything okay." I was working from home that day, so I decided to do the "I am" meditation.

As I once again went to that familiar place that I call "my Moses realm," I felt at peace, and I knew that she would be just fine. I envisioned her and my father being at my book launch, and I thought about us going out to dinner and grocery shopping like we usually do. While I was meditating, I felt that complete oneness with everything around me. I understood that all-encompassing power of the divine. I felt my soul connect with the universal energy. It scared me, but at the same time the feeling of fulfillment and joy was almost indescribable.

My mother's appointment was at 1:00 p.m., so an hour later I called my dad. He answered the phone with a cheery "yaoh," which was our little happy code for, "HI, how are you?" My heart jumped with joy because I knew right away the news was good. He didn't have to say anything else. I just knew.

I asked, "So how did it go, and where's Mom?"

"Oh, we're on our way to get lunch. Everything is perfect. Even the doctor was shocked."

This was like music to my ears. I asked him to put my mom on the phone, and her first words were, "I was so scared, but now I am relieved. Thank God." It turned out the test results were excellent. Her sugar level was where it should be. Her cholesterol was good as well, and her kidneys were functioning perfectly. She told me that her doctor was amazed and asked her what she had been doing to get these excellent results. I looked up at the ceiling and thanked God, and I thanked him again over and over even as I was talking to my parents on the phone.

As I hung up, I realized that I wasn't surprised. This just reinforced my belief in the incredible nurturing, life-saving power that could be ours if we only believed and understood how this mystery of attracting and manifesting worked. It's about connecting in a deep and meaningful way with our source and understanding the power of those words, "I am that I am."

Later that night while I was browsing on YouTube, I came across the film *The Moses Code*. The dots were connecting. It all made so much sense. I was already living *The Moses Code*, and a large part of that, I believe, had to do with me realizing my destiny. Author Michael Bernard Beckwith said something during the film that made me sit up in wonderment because it summed up everything I was feeling. Michael said, "Everyone has to come to grips with the fact that there is something calling all of us and we are presently not the person to deliver that destiny. We grow into it as we say yes to it. There is an old statement that says, 'God does not call the qualified God qualifies the called.' So when we answer that call, the presence qualifies you."

I finally got it! God is qualifying me even as I write like he is doing with so many people reading this book. You don't have to be perfect to answer your call. You just need to understand and believe in your purpose. You need to work at it little by little every day, step by step, hour by hour, or minute by minute. Rest assured that it is a work in progress. We are being qualified by God, all we need to do is say, "Yes, I am ready!" The day I understood the concept of "I am" was the day I fully and completely surrendered to my calling.

I will wake up each morning and say before I face the day, "I am that I am." Before I go to bed at night, I will remember the power that is with me every minute every step of the way. It is such a liberating feeling to know that we are connected to everyone and everything and that this connection gives us the ability to attract our hearts' desires. It also soothes our doubts and fears and brings us comfort in times of heartache and disappointment. The knowledge that we are all connected because we are all of God has to be one of the most empowering realizations we can take with us throughout our lives. I will look up at the sky, feel the grass under my feet, hear the birds sing, smell the roses, and see unconditional love in a baby's eyes, all the while remembering there is a thread connecting me and you with everything universal, a thread called God.

LESSON 2

The Soul Never Dies

I looked at his tiny body lying in the coffin and thought to myself, *I'll never see him again. He's gone forever.* The date was March 29, 1979. I was four years old, and my brother Andy, whom I loved and adored, had died. He was only fifteen months old, a little angel who came into lives for a short while but then went back to God. This was my first experience with death, with coming face-to-face with the knowledge that sometimes the people we love the most will leave us. How does a five-year-old process this? Does someone this age even have the ability to understand death?

I tried to melt into the sea of mourners around the coffin because I couldn't bear anymore to look at him in his brown suit, lying in the tiny coffin, not moving. The funeral was at my grandparents' home, and according to Hindu tradition, the body of the deceased must first be brought to the house before it was buried or cremated. As the pundit chanted the Hindu prayers, I remember feeling like I couldn't breathe. There were so many people. Where did they come from? It was the first time I ever saw my father cry, and my mother's wailing cut through me like a knife. I wanted Andy to wake up so badly. I wanted us to play together, and I needed to climb over the rails into his crib just one more time and comfort him when he cried. *Why won't he wake up?* I wondered. Then I heard someone ask, "Where is Ann Marie?"

The person who responded said, "I don't know, but she'll be okay. She doesn't know what death is."

To this day I remember that conversation. My little heart wanted to burst, and I felt so angry! How dare that person say that I didn't know what death was! My darling brother was gone forever, and yes, I knew that he had died. I knew that I would never again hear his laughter or his voice calling out to my dad and saying, "Dada." I couldn't take it anymore and edged my way out of the crowd and ran to the back of the house. There was no one there, and I curled up in a corner and cried. I don't remember who it was. Eventually someone came looking for me, and I hastily dried the tears because I was embarrassed to be seen crying. I remember thinking, *Mommy and Daddy can't see me crying because they will cry more.*

A week earlier Andy started vomiting, and within a few hours the diarrhea set in. After we rushed him to the doctor the day after he had developed the symptoms, my parents worst fears were confirmed. Their little baby boy had gastroenteritis, an infection of the stomach and bowel. In that year there was an outbreak of the disease in Trinidad, and children were especially vulnerable. Andy was admitted to hospital the day after he was diagnosed but we never would have thought that he was ill enough to die. Two days later my parents walked into the hospital ward to visit him and were told by the doctor, "I'm sorry. Your son didn't make it." My parents had a difficult time coping, and to this day thirty-four years later I know they still think about him. What would he have turned out to be? What would he have looked like as an adult? I imagine that he would have been tall and handsome and maybe an attorney.

The night he died I also became ill and started vomiting, The diarrhea followed, and I, too, was rushed to hospital while my parents tried to cope with the loss of their son and plan a funeral. In between the bouts of vomiting and diarrhea, all I could think about what that I would never see my darling brother again.

Thirty four years later I finally understand. He had served his purpose. In the fifteen months he was on this earth, he brought my family closer than we had ever been. He also had a role to play in my life, and he was helping to set the stage for my own spiritual growth. It was only when I understood and accepted that every living creature has a soul that is part of one universal energy that I finally let go of my grief. I live with the knowledge that Andy is around me and I can connect with him whenever I want to.

Do you believe in guardian angels? I do because I know Andy is one of mine. I feel him around me every day, and I feel his presence by my side, especially during those dark periods. Like that night someone tried to break into my home with the intention of killing my parents and me. God was there in our presence as was Andy, surrounding us with a shield that no evil could penetrate. My grandmother Rosie, my mother's mother, is also one of my guardian angels. I can't explain this feeling. I just know. She died when I was fourteen, and she was only fifty-six. But I have never stopped sensing her presence around me.

For most of my life I felt cheated that my brother and my grandmother had been taken from me too soon. This has changed though, and I finally found peace when I changed the lenses. I wasn't cheated at all. I was blessed! Imagine having your brother and your grandmother as angels. It makes me smile every time I think about it. This awareness also helped me resolve my relationship with my half brothers and sisters. I used to feel guilt about getting close to them emotionally. Now I accept that they are as much a part of me and vice versa as Andy was.

I'm also no longer afraid to die because I am comforted in knowing that the soul really does live forever. The energy that is the soul just passes to another energetic field, whether you believe in nirvana or heaven, whatever your definition of that realm of eternity. How about holding on to that thought that this part of us, the soul, will live forever? Andy's spirit is next to me as I write, and I believe he wants me to tell you that if you have lost a child, parent, or someone you love, they never truly leave us. You see, the soul never dies.

Remember Who Walks beside You Every Step of the Way

My first actual connection to the power of the divine must have happened when I was about sixteen years old. I was in high school and struggling with issues not uncommon for teenagers. I was overweight and felt like I wasn't as bright as some of the other girls in my class. There were only girls at my school, and discipline was intense. Girls were expected to be ladylike, accomplished, and good homemakers and many of the lessons I learnt then helped me immensely later in life.

However, those days were bittersweet—schoolgirl crushes on guys who wouldn't look twice in my direction, trying to fit in among girls who were insanely intelligent, many of them attractive and perky. Every day I went home to parents, who were struggling to make it in life and who very often had to scrape together change so that I could have money for school the next day.

I'm not quite sure how I stumbled upon the book *The Power of Positive Thinking* by Norman Vincent Peale. It may have been in the school library. I remember picking up that tattered book for the first time and reading the title with interest. I had never read a motivational book before. In fact, I had no idea they even existed. This book, however, would change my life forever. I was introduced at fifteen to the theory that we could attract whatever we wanted into our lives through positive thinking. I knew nothing about energy and vibrational theory. I simply accepted that if I focused on whatever I wanted, it would appear or happen. I gave no thought to how it would happen or why, and I convinced myself beyond a shadow of a doubt that positive thinking would never fail.

Oh, if only adults could adopt this childish blind faith in what could be or what is. Instead we are tainted by disappointment and heartache. The result is a limited belief and one that very often requires some kind of proof to win us over. Whenever I doubt, I try to go back to that time when I trusted in the power of my existence, when I didn't question or analyze too much but instead just accepted that my wishes and prayers were already being answered.

I can still recall the immense hope I suddenly felt when I began reading *The Power of Positive Thinking*. I had since childhood trusted and believed in God, but I had never actually realized that I could play a role in what could happen in my life. The combination of my Christian and Hindu upbringing was invaluable to me, but my understanding earlier in my life was that there was a God in the sky who dished out favors as he saw fit. Norman Vincent Peale completely shifted the axis of my belief. For a teenager who had big dreams but wasn't sure how on earth to go after them, this book gave me the sustenance I needed.

One of the most profound statements I read in the book has stayed with me my entire life. The quote read, "Throw your heart over the bar and the rest will follow." I remember this every time I'm in doubt, when I'm not sure if I will succeed, when I feel discouraged and scared. I throw my heart over the bar, and I *know* and trust that everything else will fall into place.

I look back at that time in my life when I discovered Norman Vincent Peale, and it makes so much sense why I had such a profound attraction to his philosophies and teachings at that age. My spirit knew that twenty-five years down the road I would be on a personal growth path that would involve inspiring others.

Even at that time my spirit was already coming home to rest. It is the same I believe with most people. There is an internal knowing that we tend to pay little attention to.

If I were to map out my spiritual path, I would go all the way back to when I was around six or seven, attending an all-girls Catholic school. I loved saying the rosary, and I thought the hymns were absolutely beautiful! I went to that school until I was eleven, and it was here that I believe I first came to know God. I was Hindu, but I felt like an outcast in school, especially when I heard the other girls talking about going to church on Sunday or attending Sunday school. There were even times when I pretended to be Catholic because I so desperately wanted to be labeled a Christian. There was a weekly mass that was held at the nearby Catholic church, and this was one of the highlights of my week. During my last year at the school many of my classmates had to be confirmed, which meant that they had accepted responsibility for their faith and destiny. Oh, how I envied this rite of passage! I couldn't understand why my parents had to be Hindu. I loved Jesus, and I wanted to be close to him. Besides I was convinced if I wasn't baptized, I would go straight to hell when I died. I even thought about being a nun.

My faith in God was unwavering. Nothing and no one could convince me that he wasn't by my side, walking with me every step of the way. Growing up was confusing in terms of my religious beliefs. I loved Christianity and held on to the concept of a God in the sky with a long, flowing beard. Christmas brought me so much joy, and the thought of Jesus as a baby and how he came into this world was the most miraculous story I had ever heard.

Then there was the other side of my life, the *pujas* (Hindu prayers) and celebrating Divali, the Hindu festival of lights. I was moved by the

Christian hymns, but the Hindu devotional songs or *bhajans* also stirred something deep within me. Hinduism also represented a connection to my culture and my Indian heritage, and I associated it with my family and where I came from. My time line in terms of religion went something like this: From birth to five years old, I had a Hindu upbringing. From five to eleven, there was a strong Catholic influence in my life because of school but at home I was surrounded by Hindu traditions and practices. From eleven to sixteen, the exposure to Hinduism was intensified because of the school I attended. (I went to a Hindu girls high school.) In addition, I spent a great deal of time with relatives who were Presbyterian. At fourteen I converted to Presbyterianism but still prayed the rosary. Between the ages of eleven to sixteen, my life was a somewhat confusing combination of Hinduism, Catholicism, and Presbyterianism.

So here I was, born a Hindu, wanting really to be Catholic, converted to Presbyterianism, believing in Mother Lakshmi (Hindu goddess), praying the rosary, celebrating Christmas and Divali, and I attended a Presbyterian church on Sundays. Even writing all of this is confusing, but it brings so much clarity as to where I am today in terms of understanding God.

I have accepted fully that God or the Creator is an unseen but strongly felt energy that we are all connected to and a part of. This energy is our source from which we came and to which we shall return when we die physically. It is inside of every living creature. It is us, and we are it. When we hurt others, we hurt God, and when others are unkind to us, it is really God they are mistreating.

A few minutes before I wrote this chapter, I felt hurt by someone I was once very close to. The person did something that made me feel unwanted and rejected. I closed my eyes and let the tears flow, but then I felt comforted by the God presence. It was as if a voice was comforting me—not really an audible voice but one that you hear within. "Don't worry, child. I see your tears and your pain."

This is the presence that I know walks with me every day, and it is this force that is by your side as well. We label it as Mother Lakshmi, Ram, Jesus, the Holy Spirit, Allah, Buddha, the Tao. It is one energy, a unified goodness that is ours to draw on in times of need. Every time I feel scared or insecure, I think about that beautiful saying from *A Course in Miracles*, which I first heard Dr. Dyer refer to with the following statement: "If you knew who walked beside at all times, on this path that you have chosen, you could never experience fear of doubt again."

My friends, I pray that whatever your religious belief, you walk secure in the knowledge that you have a spiritual backup whose reserves will never diminish. When you feel like you can't go on, this force is there. It doesn't matter what you call it. It is there. When I am in need of guidance and strength, I sit quietly and meditate on the connection we have with God energy. Know that you are never alone and understand that in those times when you feel you can't go on, this force is yours to hold on to.

I Have within Me the Ability to Heal Myself

"Dear Diary, I had half of an orange today, and I feel like I had too much to eat." That was how I started my journal entry on June 5, 1991. Twenty-three years later it is painful to read those words and even more difficult to write about that period of my life. That experience is like being in a dark pit that you know you have to climb out but have no idea how to. I didn't know it at the time; however, I was suffering from anorexia, and I was slowly killing myself. I didn't even know at the time that there was something called an eating disorder. That year was a confusing time for me and everyone around me, especially my parents and friends. No one understood what was going on in my head and in my world, and no one knew how to help me.

As a teenager, I was overweight. At sixteen I was probably close to 180 pounds at a height of five-foot-one. I was chubby as a child, and by the time I entered my teens, the weight began to pile on. Food was my comfort, and I craved sugary drinks and everything that tasted good but was really bad for me. In high school I excelled academically, and when I look back at those years, I realize that was my way for making up for what I believed was my unattractiveness. I remember having crushes on guys, and I was despondent when I was rejected. I was repeatedly called fat by the girls in high school, and one day I overheard one of my relatives say "I was "as fat as a tyre". The more weight I put on, the more I ate, and I felt good only when I was eating. One day I started having pains in my stomach and eventually had to visit the doctor. It turns out I had colic, but I could see the look of disgust on his face that I was so overweight at seventeen. His words to me were, "You are killing yourself slowly. Do you want to die?" I left his office shaken and scared. My one thought was, *I am going to lose this weight fast and show everyone!*

After that visit to the doctor I honestly believed that I could die soon, and I was terrified. I don't remember exactly how I started almost starving myself, but just as food was my addiction, depriving myself of it quickly became an obsession. Within the space of a few weeks, the weight started to drop off, and I was ecstatic!

Suddenly food became the enemy, and the thought of eating repulsed me. If I felt full, I was upset and became agitated. At that time I started my first job, and most days my mother would pack me a lunch bag; however, I would throw it in the garbage and lie and tell her I had eaten all of it. While I was at home, I tried every trick in the book to convince my parents that I was eating, but eventually they caught on. Those were tension-filled days in my home with endless shouting and yelling because my parents didn't understand what was taking place. They were just seeing their daughter gradually wilt away in front their eyes, and there was nothing they could do to make me eat.

I lost about seventy pounds in eleven months, and when I looked at myself in the mirror, all I could see was someone who was fat and unattractive. At 110 pounds I felt like I was still the person I was physically at 180 pounds. My health soon began to suffer, and my first real scare came when I tried to exercise at a gym.

That day I almost blacked out, and I would have thrown up if there had been anything in my stomach. There was one time I looked at my nails and realized that they seemed discolored with a blushing tinge. Then came the dizziness and headaches, and I felt some cold sweats during the day. I had long black, thick hair down to my waist, and soon it began falling out, getting thinner and thinner by the day. I knew that I was in a very dangerous place, but I just didn't know how to begin eating as a normal person would. I was so very terrified that I would put on the weight and that people once again laugh at me. The dizzy, light-headed feeling got worse, and there came a day I couldn't get out of bed. I was back at the doctor's office, and this time I was severely anemic with an iron deficiency. He gave me an iron shot and then instructed that I needed to receive regular shots until my iron was back to normal. I was also put on iron supplements and a special diet.

The doctor also recognized that I wasn't eating and reprimanded me for starving myself. I almost became angry that I was being forced to eat. A few days after the doctor's visit I was feeling better, and I thought, *Okay, well, this isn't so bad. I can still not eat, and I'll be okay.* That morning in the shower I decided to wash my hair, and I could remember the horror I felt when an entire clump of my hair came out in my hand as I was shampooing my head. I looked down at the tiles and saw dozens of strands of hair that had fallen as I was shampooing. A year before I was killing myself because I was eating too much. Now I was doing the same by starving. Again exactly how my recovery began is a blur, but I just knew that I had to fight the urge to starve myself. I knew that my body would begin to shut down soon, and somehow I had to climb out of that pit.

Every day was a struggle, but eventually my eating habits became almost normal. However, for years I found myself oftentimes dangerously close to once again slipping back into that self-destructive mind-set. I developed a conveyor-belt thinking process where I was able to see my thoughts about food almost like I was another person looking in from the outside. When I noticed my destructive thought patterns about food, I gave myself a mental shake and grabbed those thoughts off the belt.

Years later I eventually came across the term anorexia nervosa. First I was horrified. Then I felt rather proud of myself that I was able to get out of that dangerous spiral that I was in. I found out that eating disorders have the highest mortality rate of any mental illness. What is also shocking is that 5 to 10 percent of anorexics die within ten years of developing the disorder. Eighteen to 20 percent will be dead after twenty years, and only 30 to 40 percent ever fully recover. So too, 20 percent of people suffering from anorexia will prematurely die from complications related to their eating disorder, including suicide and heart problems.

Today I am only too aware of the signs of the times when someone is suffering from an eating disorder. A few hours before I started writing this chapter, I was speaking with someone I recognized immediately as suffering from one. She was very thin and pale, and she had thinning hair. "How are you?" I asked.

She responded, "Oh, I'm doing well. It's just that I can't keep anything in my stomach. I have this weird sickness that makes me throw up everything I eat."

So what do I say to this twenty-year-old woman? I gave her a searching look that said, "I know what's going on here." I wish I could help her, but for the time being I know that I have to adopt an approach of inaction. Years ago I would have confronted her, but I've realized that this doesn't work most times. I can, however, send her light and love and be her friend.

People ask me all the time, "How did you do it?" I honestly still don't quite know how to explain it. I believe that we all have within us our very own personal spiritual therapist. I wasn't able to get professional help at the time, but it was as if part of my soul stepped in to save me. I was able to change my thoughts somehow, and this is what I believed made that life-changing difference. I almost reached that point of no return, and somehow I subconsciously recognized that I had to help myself. I don't profess to be a healer, a prophet, or a spiritual master, but I try to emulate the energy that I know they send out to heal others. I am amazed at some instances of healing like those that are done by John of God, the controversial faith healer from Brazil. After I heard about the experiences of Oprah Winfrey and Dr. Dyer, it is difficult for me not to believe. John of God is said to perform surgeries in an effort to help the sick and dying. He says that he is a spiritual medium and his body incorporates the spirits of deceased healers.

Indeed there is still so much that can't be explained. It is precisely because I have no explanation as to how and why I healed my eating disorder that I can now write this chapter and remain convinced that we really do have the ability to heal ourselves of anything. If we believe that someone else has that ability, shouldn't it be just a matter of tapping into the energy source? When I pray for someone to be healed, I imagine a fog or mist surrounding them and me and engulfing us in its comforting embrace. I create a mental picture of the person sleeping or working or maybe driving a car, and I visualise white light surrounding him or her. The same light is around me, and this is how I send the person healing. I do so by transferring my energy to him or her. I've sometimes thought that when I was going through my eating disorder, someone was also sending me healing light. That was quite possibly one of the most trying periods of my life, but through it all, I never stopped praying. I never forgot that I had within and beside me a power that is greater than anything we could ever imagine.

LESSON 5

Anything and Everything Is Possible

E very dream starts in our hearts, and it is the visions we commit to which determine our reality. I didn't see life's circumstances or social status as a deterrent to what I wanted to achieve in life, I just knew that I would one day be on television. It was a knowing that came from deep within. It was as if my career in media was predetermined, and all I needed to do was go along with the plan that had already been set out possibly before I was even born.

"Come, Ann Marie. Come and see, Francesca!" I must have been about fourteen years old, and every evening at seven o'clock, I would find myself in front of our little black-and-white TV, waiting anxiously for the only TV newscast at the time. In the early 80s, the island had one television station—Trinidad and Tobago Television or TTT. Panorama news was the single television newscast and was a highlight of the day for many people. Francesca Hawkins was one of the newscasters and was a superstar in my eyes. I would look at her read the news, with her flawless white skin, blond hair, and beautiful eyes, and say to myself, "One day I want to do what she is doing."

At the time my parents and I lived in a tiny apartment that was almost like an annex. It was connected to the main house, which belonged to my aunt and uncle. The annex was constructed hastily for my family after we were forced to leave the even smaller house we had been renting for most of my childhood. There were no windows, no air-conditioning. The roof leaked when it rained, and it was unbearably hot during the daytime. The bedroom floors were wooden, but the planks were so rotted in some places that we had to be careful where we walked. However, it was home, and my parents made it as comfortable as they possibly could.

My memories of this time in my life are more of feelings than of actual events. This was the time of my life when the realization came that there was much more to life than what I was experiencing. This is when I began to awaken to criticism and ridicule, and I understood for the first time that social status sometimes determines how we are viewed by people. Along with this awakening came one of my life's greatest lessons, and it was taught to me by my parents. I had to be content with whatever I had and grateful for everything.

I had relatives who were wealthy. They drove expensive cars. Their children had the best of whatever money could buy, but my mom and dad would repeatedly say to me, "Ann Marie, don't worry with what you see others have. When you get older and you start working, things will get better for us."

I often think about an incident that took place when I was fifteen. It was my birthday, but I knew that having a party or celebrating wasn't possible since money was tight. I got home from school, feeling just a little bit down but not overly worried or disappointed. Then I remembered that I had a piggy bank that probably had some money in it. I waited excitedly for my dad to get home from work, and we broke it open. It turned out that I had seventeen dollars in there, which was enough for us to buy some extra groceries that evening.

Every year since then, on my birthday I remember that day, but I no longer think, *Why did we have to go through that?* Instead I now say, "Thank you, God, for blessing me with those precious moments because I now appreciate even more everything that the universe has given to me."

Those were the days I was filled with a burning desire to become a success in life. My childish brain thought, *If I made enough money, then my parents would never again have to worry about buying food.* I also wanted to buy them a house with a new roof so that they wouldn't get wet if it rained.

We really do have indomitable spirits inside all of us to accomplish whatever our hearts desire. I didn't for one moment think when I was looking at the seven-o'clock TV newscast years ago that maybe I wouldn't succeed. I refused to believe anyone who told me I couldn't do it.

I graduated from high school when I was sixteen years old, scared but excited about what lay ahead of me. Most of my friends were going on to advanced-level secondary education, which is the prelude to university in my country. I wasn't able to because at the time it was more important for me to work and assist my parents financially. I figured all I needed to do was somehow start working at a TV station. Any job I could get I would take. I just needed to get my foot in the door.

Like with everything else, nothing happens before its time. I was seventeen when I started working with a local bank, and while I hated it and it didn't pay much, I was able to help out financially with the bills at home. My first monthly paycheck was a momentous occasion—twelve hundred Trinidad and Tobago dollars (US $200.00). I worked with the bank for a year, but it was such a torturous time of my life, so I had many internal conflicts and feelings of self-doubt; however, I kept my dream firmly in sight. I knew that period of my life was a stepping stone to bigger and better things. I had no idea at that time what visualization and manifesting was, but I was doing it. I have no doubt today that each person has the ability to do the same and transform wishes into reality.

My lucky media break came at eighteen when I won a competition on a radio station. The day I went into the station to collect my prize was exhilarating. It was the first time I had ever been at a radio station, and I wasn't about to let the opportunity go to waste. I was fortunate to meet the news director, and I boldly stated my intention of wanting to be a reporter. Oh, the courage that childlike faith gives you! I had no experience or formal training in media, but strangely I never saw this as a deterrent. I just knew what I wanted, and I refused to let anyone or anything pull me away from my goal. Surprisingly the News Director asked me if I would like to come into the station on weekends and observe what happens in a newsroom. Of course I said yes, and I was soon helping the reporters as they went about gathering information and putting together the news stories. A few months later I was offered the job of writing news copy.

I had to get to work for 5:30 a.m. I had no car, and during that time my father also didn't have a car. There was no choice but for me to use public transportation. We lived in what was considered a crime-ridden area of East Trinidad in a small two-bedroom apartment. Every morning at 4:15, when most people were asleep, my father and I would walk through the darkened streets to get to where I would take the bus. We were very quiet as we walked. I was scared sometimes, and I know he was uneasy; however, he never let me see it. He had in his hand a cutlass which is a heavy sword similar to a machete, wrapped in newspapers. Some days it rained, and my dad would hold the umbrella over my head, sheltering me as we walked. To this day he remains my protector and him holding the umbrella to shelter me from the rain is an analogy of our relationship over the years.

The station where I worked in thosedays had the CNN and BBC television news feeds, which I watched during every spare moment I had, and this is how I learned to present the news. I would sit in front of the TV monitor at the station after I finished putting together the copy for the 6:00 a.m. newscast and make little notes based on what I was seeing. If the journalist was reporting on someone being murdered, I looked closely at the body language and the expressions on his or her face, and I paid careful attention to pronunciation.

Six years later after I had worked with three other media houses, I ended up at Trinidad and Tobago Television. I had already won a major regional award for excellence in journalism, the Caribbean Broadcasting Award. I was hosting live TV broadcasts, early morning programs, magazine talk shows, and women's programs. I was also reporting and sometimes producing. I was deep into broadcast media and living my life for the next big news story or event.

In 2003 I asked to anchor the Panorama evening newscast, the very same program I used to look at as a child. The big day came, and I thought I would pass out because I was so nervous! Did I get enough training? Would I stumble with the words? What if the teleprompter failed? Did I look okay? Was my makeup too much? I looked behind me at the backdrop, which said, "Panorama," and it all seemed so surreal. I looked down at my scripts and then at the two cameras in front of me. My heart was pounding so hard! I glanced again behind me and looked up at the spotlights. The director asked, "Ready, Ann Marie?" I nodded, and the countdown began. I pictured my mom and dad watching at home, and I said a prayer. "Thank you, God. I'm here. I did it."

I eventually ended up teaching broadcast journalism, and I could very often see on the faces of my students the self-doubt. I understood and could relate to their insecurities, but I would say to them, "If I could do it, you can as well." I've thought about the synergy with Dr. Dyer's life. He beat some incredible odds to become the success he is today. Who would have thought that a young boy who spent several years in foster homes would today be one of the most spiritually influential people in the world?

That first day on the Panorama set was one of the many examples in my life of the power of believing. I went on to win other awards, including Luminary of Journalism, and as I walked across the stage that night to collect my award, I again reminisced about the days when I sat in front of that black-and-white TV. My dreams became reality because I had childlike faith, I believed that I would achieve everything my heart desired. I held on to a vision, to God and to a feeling, and I refused to let go. My media journey is only part of my story, but it is a testimony that I hope will fill your heart with the knowledge that you *can* get that job, that relationship, good health, etc. Just accept that you are connected to that which makes everything possible and believe that dreams do come true.

LESSON 6

We Are Strong and Can Survive Anything!

I t's July 8, 2013, and as Tropical Storm Chantal races through the Lesser Antilles, I can't help but remember that time nine years ago when Hurricane Ivan ravaged the Caribbean. Every time I think of that time in my life, I realize that we all have in us the ability to pick up the pieces and keep going. There is another profound lesson though, and that is that we really are our brothers' keepers. As I write, I'm regularly monitoring social media to get updates on Chantal's path, and the last advisory stated that it was heading toward Barbados, St. Lucia, St. Vincent, and some of the other smaller islands. Trinidad and Tobago is not in its path but could be affected by the feeder bands of the storm. The National Hurricane Center in Miami is also sending out regular updates, and my FB news feed is filled with messages from persons throughout the Caribbean urging one another to be safe.

In the midst of all of this, I'm thinking about how there is so much beauty in caring for each other. Indeed we may quarrel among ourselves, but in times like these when we're all faced with the threat of a crisis, we have come together in a show of solidarity and support. Isn't this how it should be every day not only when it comes to countries and islands but individuals? I'm reminded of the following Native American proverb: "No tree has branches so foolish as to fight among themselves."

In 2004 when Hurricane Ivan passed through the Caribbean, I was a reporter with Trinidad and Tobago Television and was at the peak of my media career. Ivan was the strongest hurricane of the 2004 Atlantic hurricane season. It was the sixth most intense Atlantic hurricane on record. The storm almost completely destroyed Grenada and caused heavy damage to Jamaica, Grand Cayman, and the western tip of Cuba.

As the storm approached the Caribbean, I was as concerned as everyone else about our safety, but at the same time there was almost a perverse excitement that I may have to be out in dangerous weather to report on what was taking place.

Ivan narrowly missed Trinidad and Tobago, but unfortunately it devastated Grenada and Jamaica. As my colleagues and I monitored the storm from the newsroom of the TV station, it was soon apparent that Grenada was in a lot of trouble. There was no telephone contact. The TV and radio stations were off the air, and the airport was closed. News of the aftermath was slow in reaching us, but within a few hours it was clear that chaos reigned on the small island.

There were rumors that Grenada's prison had been destroyed and that the prisoners had escaped. There was no power throughout the entire island, and the protective services were under immense pressure to maintain law and order. Thousands of homes had been destroyed, and most of the hotels had also suffered damage. My boss at the time decided that the station needed to send a crew to Grenada, one reporter and a camera person.

It would be a challenging assignment for the news crew since we had no idea what would face us. The crew also would have to go by boat because the airport was closed. There would possibly be no phone contact, and it was uncertain whether any hotels were operational. We had been told that the Grenada government had declared a state of emergency and that a curfew was in effect.

We assembled in the newsroom and awaited word on which crew would be heading out to the island in the next couple of hours. I can still remember the shock on the faces of my colleagues when it was announced that I would be the reporter going to Grenada.

How on earth was I going to tell my parents that I was about to go into what could be a dangerous situation with possibly no phone contact? Surprisingly they took it well, and again when I think back to that moment, I realize that my parents have supported me in everything I have ever done even when they had misgivings.

As I said good-bye to parents that evening, my heart was racing, and I was nervous, not because of the potential danger. I was anxious to get the job done and prove that I could do it. I had never been in a situation like this before. Most journalists think about that moment in their careers when they can perform some kind of Herculean task and establish themselves as true champions of the people and the profession. Well, this was my chance, and I wanted to prove that I had what it took to be a journalist. My thoughts and actions at the time were indicative of my mission in life and said a lot about what I thought was important. I had to constantly prove to everyone that I was worthy because it was the opinion of others that validated who I was.

So I prepared myself for possibly one of the biggest adventures of my life and set off to catch the coast guard boat that would take me, my cameraman, and about a dozen other reporters to Grenada. It was to be a long night of waiting. We waited about twelve hours on the pier while the boat was loaded with relief supplies.

As the sun rose the next morning we finally set sail. The couple of hours we spent at sea on that boat were some of the most awful I have ever experienced. I vomited for most the journey. The waters were extremely choppy, and to make things worse, I got seasick very easily.

Eventually we got to Grenada, and yes, it was as bad as we had imagined. As the boat docked, one could tell immediately that this tiny island was in a state of ruin. There was a strange stillness in the air as we got off the boat. My legs were shaking, and my stomach was still churning from the rough seas. It was hot and stifling. A coast guard officer announced to our group that we were now on our own since they had to head back to Trinidad after they unloaded the boat. I looked at him in amazement. For some reason I thought they would have stayed with us. He cautioned us about being careful and reminded us that the curfew began at 6:00 p.m.

As my colleagues and I picked up our bags and made our way into the streets of St. George's, the capital, all I could think of was my parents in Trinidad. They had no way of knowing what was happening with me. I knew that I had to be safe for them.

That first day was harrowing. The group of us found ourselves at 5:30 p.m. on the streets with nowhere to go. With the curfew just thirty minutes away, panic began to set it. There were no police officers, and I was uneasy about the prisoners who were supposedly roaming about freely. We decided to keep walking, hoping to find shelter. Then we heard a most welcome sound. A car came speeding by and suddenly screeched to a halt. The occupants happened to be from Trinidad. They were security personnel from a Caribbean bank. They had come over before Ivan to secure the bank. They turned out to be angels in disguise. They were able to arrange an army escort for us and helped us find shelter in a hotel that had not been completely destroyed.

We spent three adventure-filled days in Grenada, during which time I was able to find the prime minister of the island and interview him. Miraculously on the second day my cameraperson and I were able to find a phone that was functioning. The phone was in a bank that we decided to explore. There was shattered glass everywhere, and most of the furniture was waterlogged. But as we made our way through the leaves and paper on the floor, we noticed what appeared to be a fax machine with blinking lights on it. This was to be our link to the outside world.

That afternoon I was able to send a story back to the station with an update from the Grenada government. My parents also could now breathe easy because I was okay. I spoke to scores of Grenadians during those couple of days, and what I saw frightened me. The immense force of Mother Nature and our vulnerability as human beings was undeniable. Would Grenada ever pick itself up after Ivan? How would people survive with an economy that was struggling even before the hurricane?

Three days after I first arrived in Grenada, we got word that the airport had reopened, and we decided to try our luck in getting back to Trinidad. When we got to the airport, it was chaotic but partially functioning. Foreigners and tourists who were not able to get out before the hurricane were now frantically trying to leave the island.

My cameraperson and I were luckily able to get on a flight back to Trinidad. As the plane took off from the runway, I looked down at the devastation below. I couldn't wait to get back home and tell my story, but I felt a deep sense of loss for the people of Grenada. I thought about those hundreds of families who had nowhere to sleep and the thousands of others with no jobs to go to. How would the children go to school with most of the buildings destroyed? Life seemed so fragile, but I knew that the Grenada people would survive and that the island would one day get back to where it was before Ivan. After all, isn't that the power of the human spirit? Isn't that why we are given the indomitable will to live? No matter how difficult it may seem sometimes, we all have what it takes to get to the other side. I can't tell you how many times I have said to myself, "I don't know how I would ever get through this," but I find comfort in the words of Ecclesiastes 3:1–3 (NKJV), "To everything there is a season, and a time to every purpose under the heaven: A time to be born, and a time to die; a time to plant, and a time to pluck up that which is planted; A time to kill, and a time to heal; a time to break down, and a time to build up."

Today Grenada is still coping with a struggling economy, and many people have not rebuilt their lives completely; however, they are far from where they were in 2004, when everything seemed hopeless. The island and its people are testimony that no matter how bad the situation may seem, it never lasts and that we have the capacity to start all over again.

LESSON 7

Go After What You Want Even If It Seems Impossible!

A few months into writing this book I attended a job interview and was asked by one of the persons in the panel about my most memorable interview when I was a journalist. There are a couple of them that stand out, but the one that really had an impact on me was one I did with former US President Bill Clinton. I've always felt that this episode in my life reinforced my belief in the power of going after what I wanted and keeping that vision firmly in sight. For me it is a testimony of what Johann Wolfgang Von Goethe said, "What you can do, or dream to do, begin to do. Boldness has genius, power and magic in it."

I remember that day in September 2001 I burst through the front door, anxious to tell my mother about Mr. Clinton's visit. "Mom, Mom, guess who's coming to Trinidad?" The former president was to be the guest speaker at a leadership conference in October, and as a young reporter, the news was music to my ears! Those were the days when news was "in my blood," and an interview with someone as famous as Bill Clinton would be an achievement that I thought would certainly help me mark my territory the in Trinidad and Tobago media. Oh, how I yearned to travel overseas and cover wars and interview powerful controversial politicians. I wanted to be a CNN reporter and become as famous as Christiane Amanpour. No wonder I was so excited about the Clinton visit. Talk about the mountain coming to Mohammed!

Every morning there was a newsroom meeting where the assignments of that day would be discussed. This morning it was different, there was a definite buzz as the journalists waited to hear about the Clinton assignment. I was intent on being chosen, I had to meet him, I so wanted that photo! It's not often that a president or former president of the United States visits Trinidad and Tobago, and I had to ensure that I was in on the action. Yes, I admit that I was fascinated with the Monica Lewinsky incident!

The day I told my mom about the Clinton visit, she looked at me and calmly responded, "Oh, yes, I know you will meet him."

We looked at each other knowingly, and I responded, "Yes, I will." At the time I didn't exactly know how, but I was determined that it had to happen, I wanted this so badly. How could it not happen? Have you ever longed for something with such intensity that you convince your brain that it's yours even before it has actually taken place? Well, I believe this is exactly what happened in this case. Nothing and no one could shift my intention! To this day whenever I feel like I'm faced with what may appear to be an impossible task, I go back to that time in my life and relive the emotions, the wanting, and the determination that made me stick like glue to what I wanted to accomplish.

As the days went by, it was clear that interviewing President Clinton would certainly be a challenge. The conference organizers advised newsrooms across the country about security measures and protocols that had to be adhered to during the time the former president would be in Trinidad. There would be no interviews at any time, and journalists would not be allowed anywhere near him.

Despite what seemed like an impossibility, I was not shifting from my goal, I held on to it for dear life, and I visualized that photograph of me posing with Mr. Clinton at least ten times a day. The conference received a lot of publicity, so not only were journalists hyped, but everyone else, especially the politicians and businesspersons, were also interested.

Two days before the conference I was told by my news director that I was the reporter who would represent my station at the event. I remember calmly listening to him and thinking that this didn't even come as a surprise. It was as if things were unfolding the way they were supposed to.

On the morning of the conference I got up early and spent some extra time getting dressed. I was pensive while I had my coffee. I imagined what it would feel like at the end of the day to see my story of the Clinton interview in the 7:00 p.m. newscast. When I look back at those moments, I understand why I was able to manifest what I did. I had connected to the power of intention.

As I said good-bye to my mother that morning, I told her with certainty, "I'm going to get my picture with Bill Clinton."

She said to me, "Yes, you will." I looked at her, smiled knowingly, and walked out the front door.

When I got into the newsroom, I busied myself with getting my crew together before we left for the Hilton Trinidad, where the conference was being held. I told my boss, "I'm going to get that interview for us." He laughed and shook his head almost as if he was saying, "There goes Ann Marie again."

I enjoyed every minute of that conference but could get nowhere near the president. Within minutes after his speech to a packed hall, they whisked him off to private meetings and then a luncheon with the prime minister of Trinidad and Tobago. By this time most of the other journalists and camerapersons had left after they had realized that it seemed impossible to get an interview with Mr. Clinton. I refused to give up. "We're not going anywhere," I told my cameraperson. I could see the look of annoyance on his face, but he went along. I called my boss and told him that we would hang out at the Hilton for a while longer just in case an opportunity arose. I eventually found out where the private luncheon with the prime minister was taking place, and my cameraperson and I stationed ourselves a few feet away. There was a newspaper journalist and photographer with us as well. About an hour later amidst a flurry of activity, President Clinton emerged together with the prime minister and some high-profile and very powerful businesspeople.

We were almost pushed into a corner by the security detail, and we found ourselves about twenty feet away from the winding staircase which the president and his entourage were being led to. By this time there were dozens of hotel staff members who had gathered as well, many with cameras in hand ready to take a photo of President Clinton even if it was from a distance.

The excited chatter got louder as President Clinton mounted the staircase and he looked toward the crowd that had gathered to his left but were behind the security personnel. I'm sure to this day he looked directly at me and waved, and his small gesture elicited excited chatter from the onlookers who waved back amidst the flashing lights of cameras. The group got to the top of the stairs, and I realized they were headed to the hotel lobby and possibly to a balcony overlooking the city.

The security personnel in front of us moved away and followed the entourage. I urged my cameraperson, "Let's follow them." He looked at me as if I was crazy, but we raced up the stairs in hot pursuit. The group was heading to the patio just as I had thought. We were again kept at bay by those burly security guys in dark suits.

After a few minutes the group turned to leave the patio and was directed to another staircase, and I assumed it was time for another meeting. In a split second I knew that if I didn't' act, then I would lose the only opportunity I had to meet Mr. Clinton. To this day I have no idea why this question came into my head, but I shouted from across the hotel lobby: "President Clinton, how was your lunch?"

I could see the bewilderment on the faces of the persons who were accompanying the president, including the prime minister. I could sense the trepidation in the newspersons behind me, including my own cameraperson. I said to him, "Just keep shooting." Mr. Clinton turned and looked in my direction, and then the most amazing thing happened. He was about to go down the stairs, but instead he started walking toward where I was standing. I felt my knees beginning to buckle, but my brain went into autopilot. He walked straight up to where I was standing, his entourage behind, including the prime minister. I whipped out the microphone as he greeted me with that trademark smile and responded, "Lunch was excellent." I interviewed Mr. Clinton for about five minutes on the discussions he had during lunch, which included government-to-government policies and his thoughts on the future of the relationship between the Trinidad and Tobago and the United States.

The interview ended, and I graciously thanked him for his time. Then I remembered my photo, and I made another split-second decision! It was now or never! I had to document this encounter. As he turned to leave, I boldly asked, "Excuse me, President Clinton. May I take a picture with you?" Again everyone seemed to have gone completely silent.

More shock set in when he responded, "Yes, of course." The breaches in protocol went even further as he asked one of the men in black suits to do the honors and take the picture with my camera.

A few minutes later the group turned and left the lobby. There were heading back to the staircase that would take them to their next meeting.

I had to sit for a few minutes in the hotel lobby. I was almost shaking. My own boldness shocked me, but in the end I had achieved what I had wanted because I'd refused to be intimidated by what appeared to be impossible.

That evening my station aired the story, which was "a scoop," as it is referred to in the news business. We had a story no one else had, an interview with former US President Bill Clinton.

This stands out as one of the most memorable experiences of my media career, and I go back to it whenever I feel doubt setting in. I relive the experience, the emotions, the pride, and the confidence that led to that interview taking place. When I feel insecure about anything, I look at the photo of the former president, and I say to myself, "If you did it then, you can surely do it now." I connected with the power that makes dreams become reality, a power that we all have within us. This is the same energy I draw on when I look at the photo of Dr. Dyer and me at the conference in Atlanta.

These days I don't dream about interviewing presidents, but I still hold on to the determination I had twelve years ago when I wanted that interview. I've learned to appreciate the connection we have with intention, and I so absolutely believe that anything—and I mean *anything*—is possible once we align our desires with what is good and pure and true.

LESSON 8

Trust Your Intuition. It Never Fails!

ow why would anyone who can't swim go onto a jet ski and venture into deep water? Well, that's exactly what I did and almost lost my life because I didn't have the courage to say no. I also didn't trust my intuition and the feeling deep within that said danger was around the corner. Years after the incident I'm about to relate, I have finally understood what Garvin Becker meant in his book *The Gift of Fear*.

> But it isn't just a feeling. It is a process more extraordinary and ultimately more logical in the natural order than the most fantastic computer calculation. It is our most complex cognitive process and at the same time the simplest. Intuition connects us to the natural world and to our nature. Freed from the bonds of judgment, married only to perception, it carries us to predictions we will later marvel at.

I was on vacation in Mexico with Dominic, and the weekend was going great. We left Trinidad on Friday afternoon, and as the plane landed in beautiful Cancun, I smiled to myself as I thought about the romantic, relaxing weekend I was about to have. I was twenty-five at the time and had already begun to make a name for myself in media. I met Dominic about a year earlier at a conference in Antigua. I was immediately besotted with this tall and good-looking Canadian who came riding into my life on a proverbial white horse.

The relationship was a rocky one, and the tensions were fuelled by my own sense insecurities. It was Dominic's idea to go get away for a weekend, and I welcomed the idea, thinking that it would somehow help resolve some of the relationship issues. Dominic was a daredevil in every sense of the word and insisted even before we left Trinidad that he would be renting a jet ski in Cancun whether I liked it or not. I looked at him with trepidation, hoping that he wasn't serious, silently praying that he wouldn't ask me to join him. I had no such luck. In the same breath he said, "Yeah, babe, and you're coming with me."

At twenty-five I had as yet found my own voice, my independence, and my ability to avoid being influenced by others, especially men. It was easier to go along with what he wanted than stand up for myself. It was an interesting contrast of characters. Here I was known in media circles and in the public as a strong-willed, opinionated, and courageous journalist. However, in my personal life I tended to be easily swayed and was struggling with my own independence.

We arrived in Mexico on a Friday, and during the taxi ride to the hotel Dominic again let me know that he wanted to get onto that jet ski. I asked if it was safe since he couldn't even swim. This didn't make a difference to him. He said that he had done it before and that it was quite safe. So much for hoping that he would lose interest!

Saturday passed without any more conversations about jet skis, and I began to relax, taking in the sunshine and gorgeous beaches. Sunday morning came, and after breakfast we decided to hit the beach. I sat under an umbrella with my eyes closed, and I remember thinking about my parents, wondering what they were up to. I made a mental note to call them as soon as I got back to the hotel.

I looked at Dominic lying on the sand next to me and thought about my life. Was this what I wanted? Was this man someone I wanted to spend the rest of my life with? Would he be someone my parents would even want as a son-in-law?

A few minutes later a jet ski cruised up to the beach a few feet away from us, and Dominic jumped up when he realized that the sound he was hearing was the engine. The guy on the jet ski was one of the operators, and I felt a sense of foreboding as Dominic negotiated with him on the price to rent the ski. A few minutes later he returned to where I was sitting and cheekily informed me that we were about to have the time of our lives.

I insisted that I would not be joining him, and I reminded him that I couldn't swim and that neither could he! Eventually he seemed to give up, waved to me, and jumped on the ski. I watched Dominic with interest, and I was so happy I was safe and sound on solid ground! He didn't go very far out into the water, and after about ten minutes he circled back to where I was sitting on the beach. He jumped off the ski and then proceeded once again to try to convince me to get on. "Come on … please. I promise you I'll be careful and you'll be safe. Don't you trust me?"

No, I don't trust you, was what I was thinking, but I said, "Of course I do. It's just that I don't want to right now." He didn't give up, and eventually I gave in. To this day I wonder what I was thinking and why I said yes and trusted him when deep down inside I knew that I was putting myself in danger.

Dominic helped me put the life jacket on, and I climbed on the seat, which seemed slippery. I immediately went into a panic as the jet ski took off and I realized the water was deeper than I had first thought it was. At first he went slowly, and then he picked up speed. I felt the panic increase, and I begged him to slow down. My pleas didn't make a difference though. He just ignored me. I soon realized that he racing straight out to sea, and real terror set it. I began screaming and begging him to turn back. I turned to look at the shore and realized that I could hardly even see it, and I knew that we had gone too far.

I remember this moment clearly as if it was yesterday. Dominic turned to the side and shouted, "Well, babe, if you love me, then you could die with me." About ten seconds later he made a sharp turn with the jet ski. I don't remember whether it was to the left or right, but I leaned in the opposite direction, which I wasn't supposed to do.

If ever there was an incident in my life that seemed like it happened in slow motion, then this was one of them. It is difficult even to write about this because the terror was so intense. My body hit the water, and I vaguely remember seeing Dominic topple into the ocean as well. It also isn't clear to me exactly what I held on to, but I managed to maintain my grip on the ski as it turned over.

If you are familiar with the bottom of a jet ski, then you know it is round and smooth and there isn't much to hold on to. Even as all of this was happening, I remembered that I was wearing a life jacket, and I consoled myself that I couldn't drown. It must have been a few minutes later when my arms begun to get tired and I let go of the jet ski, but to my horror I began to sink. I felt Dominic behind me, trying to hold me, but he, too, was going under. The life jackets weren't helping. (Recently someone suggested that they may not have been inflated enough. I'm not sure.)

Dominic made several attempts to turn over the jet ski; however, we were told later that if he had succeeded, then it would have just filled up with water and sunk, and we wouldn't have had anything to hold on to. I don't remember much about what we said while we were in the water, but the one thing that stays in my mind is my plea to God.

"Please help us, God. Please help us," I cried repeatedly. I couldn't see the shore, and we were in the middle of the ocean with nothing and no one in sight. My hands began to get tired. I felt my grip loosen once again, and I began to go under.

I experienced at that moment what it felt like to have your life flash before your eyes because that is what happened to me. I saw myself blowing out candles on a birthday cake as a child. There were images of me reading the news and pictures of sitting in the backseat of my father's car as a child. I also thought about my parents. Who would tell them that I had drowned in Mexico.I prayed that they would get the strength to handle the pain.

I'm not sure how long we were in the water, but out of nowhere I noticed in the distance a jet ski racing toward us. I'm uncertain as to how long it took to get to us, but this person was truly an angel sent directly from God. What happened next was a blur, the person on the jet ski helped Dominic get me on the seat behind him. We had to leave Dominic in the water because there was only room for one on the ski. He raced toward shore with me and handed me over to a group of people who were on the beach. As I lay on the beach and trembled, I tried to think about what had just happened. It seemed like my mind was too numb even to process what had taken place.

Time seemed to be standing still because I don't know how long it took the Good Samaritan to bring Dominic back to shore. I couldn't even look at Dominic as he hugged me. I was so angry, scared, and terrified. I just wanted to go home and be with my parents.

It turns out that the stranger had been some distance away but had seen our overturned jet ski and decided to investigate. It was only as he got closer did he realize that there were people in the water.

Dominic and I broke up soon after this incident, but it is one of the most significant moments in my life. To this day, I can't go into the ocean or even a swimming pool. If I am on a boat and I feel the motion of the sea, I go into a panic because I regress to that day in Mexico.

I have learned to always trust my intuition, and if I feel unsafe, I get myself out of the situation. I have often asked myself, "So why do our lives flash before our eyes at the moment we feel we are about to die?"

Since then I have often pondered on what my final thoughts would be when I say good-bye to this body. *What is the legacy that I would like to leave behind?* I don't want to have regrets or be fearful or in pain. No one should, and my heart goes out to those who do. I can't help but think of an elderly man I worked with very earlier in my career. Sometime in 2013 I heard that he had passed away in his home all by himself and that his body was only discovered days later. What was he thinking? I don't want to be alone or feel unwanted when I say good-bye to this life.

Every day is your chance to determine what our final thoughts will be. Whatever we do today, every moment will have an impact on the images we get if indeed life has to flash before our eyes.

I want to remember my parents smiling, my first kiss, the launch of this book, conversations over coffee with dear friends. These are the moments that will define my time on earth, and my hope is that yours are just as beautiful.

The Mexico incident happened when it was supposed to. It was an insight into one of our greatest gifts, our intuition.

LESSON 9

God Talks to Us in Our Moments of Desperation

"**I**f you experience that desperation that causes a man to commit suicide and you feel you cannot live without seeing God, then you will see God." These words from Dr. Wayne Dyer resonated deeply with me because I could totally relate to what he was saying. According to Dr. Dyer, this was one of the twelve ways of realizing God. It actually explains a lot of what I have been feeling and the questions I have about why I have gotten to the spiritual place where I find myself today. I had no choice but to see God and experience him in all his glory because I was at that desperation stage.

I remember lying in bed, thinking some years ago, *God, please don't let me wake up tomorrow.* Today I ask myself, "How could I even let my mind go there?" After all, I am supposed to be a sane, accomplished, supposedly strong, levelheaded woman. However, sadness, desperation, and hurt have no preferences. There are so many people whom we believe are in charge of their lives and who are going through such deep-rooted turmoil that they feel trapped in an abyss of depression. Have you noticed when people we know commit suicide, we often think, *But he seemed okay and was so happy. I never thought he would want to end his own life.*

There was a time when I felt like giving up on life, but I held on to the thought that my parents needed me and loved me. Secondly I believed that God existed, and no matter how awful and dark my world became, the Creator was always with me.

Now that I think about it, every time I got to the stage of my life—and there were several of them—God always made himself known in some form or another.

The year 2010 was a significant one for me because it was a turning point. That was when I finally decided that I would no longer allow perceived disappointment to overpower me. One night I was lying on the couch in a haze of despair. I was living in Florida at the time and just could not come to terms with the fact that my marriage was in shambles. All I could think of was how disappointed my parents would be in me and that I would embarrass them if my marriage failed.

I thought about how happy my parents were the day I got married—as painful as it was for them to know that I would soon be leaving them to live abroad. In my culture, even today it is expected most times that women get married by the time they are in their mid-twenties. In my case I was a bit of rebel, and by the time I hit thirty, I was viewed as "being on the shelf." As the years rolled by, I became increasingly dejected, even though I didn't want to admit it. Eventually I was the only one left among my cousins who was not married, and I felt like such a failure! I'm not sure when I made that very conscious decision that no matter what, I *was* going to get married. I sent out that energy, and of course the universe answered me.

So there I was that night in April 2010, lying on that couch in Florida, thinking about my spectacular wedding and the admiration on the faces of the guests. I felt like I had made such a complete mess of my marriage, and I felt utterly hopeless. At the time I was blaming myself and thinking that I wasn't good enough.

This was also a few months after that awful, horrible day when I was told at the doctor's office that I had miscarried. When I found out I was pregnant, I felt like I was in a dream. When it happened, it felt surreal, like it was somebody else's body. I greeted the first bout of morning sickness with joy. I wanted to experience every stage of being pregnant.

Then came that day in the doctor's office. The ultrasound didn't show a heartbeat, and my world came crashing down around me. One night a few months later I lay curled up on the couch, thinking, *Life is too hard. I can't do this anymore.* As I sobbed, the tears rolled down my cheeks because I felt completely and utterly dejected. Then I started to doze off, and in between that stage of being half awake and half asleep, I saw behind my closed eyelids what appeared to be line of text, and a voice seemed to be reading it to me. The voice was more of an inner knowing almost. I can't really describe it or distinguish it, but it said to me, "I will lift you up on wings of eagles, and they will know that I have done this."

I fell asleep, but the minute I opened my eyes, I remembered what I had experienced. I knew no matter what that everything was going to be okay and that one day I would once again shine. I also understood that I had a purpose to fulfill in my life and that those thoughts about giving up had to stop. I accepted then that an indescribable power was with me.

Years later I still remember that night vividly, but I have stopped asking, Why me?" I finally understand it had to be me! Just like it has to be you in whatever experience you may encounter in life. For me it's not even about good or bad experiences anymore. It's just part of my life's tapestry, which has been woven for a reason. I had to reach out to God when I was sinking. I had to raise my arms and plead with him to help me. There were days I didn't even want to pray or even believe, but that, too, was supposed to have happened so that I could understand what immense power there is out there. The most wonderful part is that it is ours to have whenever we want it! I have my eagles like you have yours. They are your angels, your salvation. They will lift you up and soar with you to heights you can't even imagine.

It Always Gets Better. Just Hold on!

My exercise in cleaning out my e-mail in-box was one that I had procrastinated doing for such a long time, but I finally decided that I had to get it done. I knew that I was hesitating and putting it off because there was a part of me that just wasn't ready to take that trip down memory lane.

The day that I finally decided to bite the bullet and tackle that in-box was a trying one. I had encountered more than one incident of rejection, and by the end of the day that familiar feeling of not being appreciated began to set it. It seemed like it was one blow after another, and I asked God silently on the drive back home from my office to please come into my heart and fill me with the peace and acceptance I needed so that I would not be affected. I was hurting for more than one reason. It was a combination of work and my personal life. That familiar hollowness in the pit of my stomach set it. The lesson that I had to learn was once again presenting itself clearly, and it was up to me to embrace the message. It was dressed in different clothing but had the same undergarments.

I felt alone and scared. Emotions that I hadn't experienced in some months came back, and I tried to figure out why they had resurfaced on this particular day. I thought that I was well on my way to mastering the feelings of rejection, but I've now accepted that wounds oftentimes appear deeper than we think they are.

I thankfully arrived home that evening from work, relieved to be out of the traffic and finally able to relax in the sanctuary of my bedroom. I quickly got out of my work clothes, slipped on a robe, and lay back in bed. The tears rolled down my face in the darkened room as I listened to a CD of bhajans (Hindu devotional songs). "Please, God," I prayed, "come into my heart and help me to keep grounded and focused enough to know that my purpose is to help others."

I thought that I had gotten past the pain of my divorce, and I realized what I was feeling was fear and panic, the feeling that I would never have a partner to stand by me when my parents had passed. I took a deep breath, and determination set it. I wiped my tears and began my tasks for that night, one of which was to write a chapter for my book, the other to clean up my in-box.

As I went through e-mail from 2008, 2009, and 2010, I tried not to reminisce, but my mind went back to those years anyway. I saw e-mail exchanges between my former mother-in-law and me, my ex-husband, friends in Florida, and family in Trinidad. Each e-mail had a memory attached to it, but I ploughed through anyway—delete, delete, delete.

Then I came across one from Christmas of 2010. It was an e-card from my ex-husband and me sent to friends and family, inviting them to our home on Christmas Eve. The card included a photo of us, and I looked at the smiling faces almost in disbelief. Was this actually my life at one time? I read the address on the card. It was our home in Florida, and I felt a deep sense of loss and disappointment; however, I told myself, though my eyes filled with tears, that this had to happen.

Interestingly, earlier that night I had asked God for a message, something to comfort me. As I usually do, I opened my Bible randomly, and on this night the page opened onto Ecclesiastes 7 (NKJV), which says in verse 13 to 14, "Consider the work of God; for who can make straight what he has made crooked? In the day of prosperity be joyful. But in the day of adversity consider; surely God has appointed the one as well as the other. So that man can find out nothing that will come after him."

I interpreted this to mean that even though I had gone through heartbreak and rejection, it would not last forever and that everlasting love could be right around the corner!

As I looked at that e-mail, I felt so much sadness, but I was determined to continue with my cleanup exercise. Then I saw one from my dear friend Kennedy, who had helped me through some of the roughest and emotionally challenging periods of my life. I saw his e-mail with the subject "This is to keep the dream in your heart," and I smiled because I felt that warmth that comes from knowing that you are loved unconditionally. I decided to click on it. This is some of what was said:

> But one day, sweet Ann Marie,
> I will want to see you dance,
> as every light turns in distraction to gaze upon your face
> instead of the world.
> I want to see you laugh and leap from the ground and
> again believe that you can touch the sky.
> Wake up, arise and believe.
> Never stop. You're a child of the cane, remember?

I sat very still and read these words again, absorbing them and marveling at the timing. Kennedy was telling me that which we all need to hold on to, namely to "wake up, arise, and believe." Oh, those words! I could almost hear Kennedy's voice encouraging me to "leap from the ground and again believe that you can touch the sky."

So what happened earlier on that day? Why did I stop believing that I could just reach up and grasp the marvelous gifts that could be mine?

I have chosen to channel my heartaches into transmitting what I like to call "hope energy." This is the energy that says, "No matter what, you have to get up this morning and give this day everything you've got." It is the energy that keeps you from giving up on your dreams, your marriage, and your children. It is that unseen force that pushes you on while you're studying for that degree, and it is what encourages you to pray when you're sick and unwell.

Hope energy is what you see in the eyes of those who love you when you can't love yourself. I draw on it, and so can you. It is like a lifesaver that is thrown out to sea when you feel like you're going under. I reach out, grab it, and hold on for dear life, and I'm encouraging you to do the same. It's always there. It's your inner voice saying, "Don't you dare give up!" If you are reading this book, then my wish is that you feel it coming directly from me to you.

LESSON 11

Our Dreams Hold the Answers

I believe that our dreams construct a compass for life. They give us supernatural insights and provide us with invaluable direction that the waking mind is sometimes incapable of seeing. I've looked back at several incidents in my lifetime that were linked to dreams, but at the time I either could not make the connection or just refused to because I wasn't ready to face the truth. I know there are endless scientific explanations as to what dreams really are. Sigmund Freud tells us, "A dream represents an ongoing wish along with the previous day's activities. They may even portray wishes that have been inside us since early childhood."

I actually quite like Edgar Cayce's take on the purpose of dreams. He believed that if you are to interpret your dreams correctly, you must thoroughly study yourself. "Once you know how you feel about dreams and what they can do for you can you begin to study your dreams." "If you have a dream," according to Cayce, "it's primary focus is to either solve problems and adapt to external affairs or awakening and alerting the dreamer to new potential within the self."

Over the years I have come to trust my dreams and to make that connection to things that are happening in my life, especially those situations that are troubling and stressful. In April 2013 I was betrayed by someone I trusted, and once again those familiar feelings of rejection and not being good enough resurfaced.

I felt so dejected and couldn't understand why. I began asking God to please show what my purpose in life really is. The conversations went something like this: "God, I don't understand. I'm trying to do the right thing. I'm living my life to serve you and help others. Dear God, I am sorry if I have hurt others in the past and myself. Please guide me, Father, but God, why do I have to feel this pain over and over again?"

I began doubting myself, and questioning whether I was even qualified to help others. I knew in my heart that I was on this earth to give others hope; however, there was no direction to my purpose, and I still felt like I had one foot in and the other foot out the door.

One night at the end of April I had a dream that changed everything. I dreamed that I was with my friend Steven and we were in a mall somewhere in the United States. We were on an escalator, and I turned, looked at him, and said, "I'm going to Atlanta to attend the Hay House conference." Then the scenes changed, and we were in a house somewhere. Again we were having a conversation. He then showed me a small rectangular brown box with a name on it, and he said to me, "Remember, you're this."

The next morning my dream was surprisingly easy to recall, and I lay in bed for about thirty minutes and thought about it. I didn't immediately recall what was written on the box, but then it came flooding back. The name on the box was "Kirsten." I jumped out of bed and wrote it down. "Kirsten?" I asked myself. "What on earth does that mean?"

Still in my pajamas I decided to google the name and see what I came up with. I typed, "What is the meaning of the name Kirsten?" What I came up with left me speechless. There in black-and-white was the definition. To this day, I get chills when I think about what I read that morning. "The name Kirsten is of Scandinavian, English, and Danish origin. The meaning of Kirsten is "follower of Christ." Another definition stated that it meant, "The anointed one, follower of Christ."

I sat on my bed, stunned, knowing that I had received a message directly from God, and despite everything that had happened in my life, my destiny was indeed to inspire and help others.

It's easy to sometimes feel lost in the crowd. I have come across so many amazing stories. For instance, Anita Morjani, who had cancer, had a near-death experience and then fully recovered from her illness. Immaculee Ilibagiza survived the Rwandan war after she hid in a bathroom with seven other women for ninety one days. Iyanla Vansant seems to be a channel through which God himself speaks. These are women I admire greatly, but when I started comparing my stories to theirs, I felt like I didn't deserve to write a book. That dream changed so much for me. It was God telling me that yes, in my own small way I, too, am a messenger of God just like so many of you reading my book are.

That dream in April 2013 confirmed what I already knew about my calling but still hadn't fully embraced. I thought back to another dream I had years ago. I dreamed then that I was present at the time of Jesus's crucifixion and was one of the hundreds who were lining the road as he carried his cross up Calvary hill. I felt like I was soaring above the scene, which seemed almost like a movie. This dream also left me shaken because in analyzing that dream afterward, I realized that I was Veronica. It is believed that she wiped the face of Christ when he fell under the weight of the cross on the way to Calvary. I actually saw myself kneeling and wiping his face and then looking at the white cloth with his face imprinted on it.

At the time I had this dream, I knew there was a powerful message attached, but then I dismissed it. Simply put, I was afraid to acknowledge it. Five years later the message came to me again in another dream, but this time I owned up to the fact that I was Kirsten, a follower of Christ. There are so many Kirstens out there who are afraid to say, "Yes, God, I hear you."

Now I understand that dreams are the gateway through which we can really get close to God and to understanding ourselves. My friend Shivana and I have had long talks about the significance of our dreams, and we both agree that this time is when we travel through various dimensions. This is when we can actually connect with our soul mates and receive messages that we are meant to share with the rest of humanity. Interestingly, we now understand a lot more about ourselves after we have analyzed our dreams. For instance, we have accepted that we are soul mates and that at some time during our spiritual journey, we were both living close to the ocean. Shivana and I continue to have dreams about floods, tidal waves and drowning. This has led us to believe that we may have both drowned at some time in a previous life and that we quite possibly lived in the same village. I've often asked myself if this is why I may have a never-ending fear of the ocean.

I try to be cautious about interpreting dreams, but I believe that if we have placed serving God and others as our number-one priority and we ask for the answers in our dreams, then indeed while we sleep we will receive our instructions.

The Bible teaches that in ancient times God relayed his messages through the power of the Holy Spirit to his chosen servants by visions and dreams. These messages were also given to the apostles and prophets. Buddhists in India believe that some dreams are messages or teachings from God. I do agree with the psychological explanation that our daily activities (while we are awake) can have an effect on our dreams, but in the same breath I believe the spiritual logic. Indeed the answers from the universe and messages from God definitely can be channeled through us in our dreams. As is stated in Job 33:15–16, "In a dream, in a vision of the night, when deep sleep falls upon men.

While slumbering on their beds. Then he opens the ears of men, and seals their instruction."(NKJV)

The universe continues to calm my insecurities and fears in my dreams, and these days I'm excited about going to sleep. Who knows what will happen when I enter dreamland! In fact, there are some mornings when I wake up and I'm disappointed because I didn't have any dreams. Our dreams are another element of our life's journey and they certainly hold the answers to many of the questions we may have along the way.

LESSON 12

Keep on Believing in Miracles!

Here's a story that I would like to share because every time I remember this incident, I say to myself, "Well, God, if ever I wanted proof, here it is."

It was a sunny Sunday morning in March 2012, and I was all fired up about a broadcasting class I was about to teach. As I dressed, I prayed that the class would go well and that I would inspire my students to recognize their true potential. The interesting thing about the classes I taught, which was broadcast journalism, was that most of the students seemed unsure at first about whether they had made the right choice. My goal was simple—motivate them, give them hope, and encourage them to believe in themselves. Each group was different. Some were more complicated than others, but I took it all in stride, knowing that some would heed the advice I gave them and others would just go back out into the world, locked in their self-limiting beliefs.

This particular class was new. I hadn't met them before, so I didn't know what to expect. As I climbed the stairs to the first floor of the building, I prayed that I would do and say the right things. I took a deep breath before I entered the classroom because the four hours or so I usually spent teaching were grueling.

As with all of the introductory class sessions, I took some time to get to know the new group. I told them a little bit about myself and then invited them to say something about themselves. The last person to speak was a young lady I had noticed almost from the moment I entered the room. She was sitting in the back row. She was thin and looked malnourished. Her hair was unkempt. She wore no makeup. She was wearning an old pair of jeans and a top that looked way too big for her. She sat with her arms folded, looking down at the floor for most of the time. I recognized right away that something was not right. She was almost trying to melt into the wall behind her, and she wouldn't look at me while I was speaking.

Eventually it was her turn to speak, and the class looked at her expectedly. At first I could hardly hear a word she was saying, so I asked her to speak up. Her name was Sandra, and she said she was in the class because her parents felt it would help her to "come out of her shell." She was eighteen years old, but she looked like she was twelve. She spoke with a tone of uncertainty, as though she wasn't sure if she was allowed to speak. Then she told us a most shocking story, one that wasn't at all expected, especially since all the people in the class were strangers to one another.

Sandra lived in a remote village in East Trinidad. She had parents who were hard working and who recognized the value of education. Two years ago Sandra got up one morning, dressed for school, said good-bye to her parents, and entered a neighbour's car to be taken to school.

This was routine, and the neighbor, a kindly woman in her forties, was happy to assist. This morning, however, the woman wasn't driving when the car pulled up. Her teenaged son was in driver's seat.

The woman had fallen ill that morning, so her son had agreed to drop off Sandra to school. There was hush in the room as Sandra spoke. We all knew that what we were about to hear was no ordinary story. She bent her head, and her hair fell in front of her face as she continued. Her hands lay folded in her lap, and her lips quivered slightly. Sandra told us she felt uncomfortable the moment she entered the car, but she dismissed the feeling. Little did she know that her life was about to change forever.

The young man never took her to school, but instead he drove to an abandoned house about twenty minutes from Sandra's home, dragged her into the house at 8:00 a.m. in the morning, and repeatedly raped her at knifepoint.

Two hours later Sandra made her way home and told her mother that the exam she was supposed to have done at school had been postponed. According to Sandra, she showered about ten times that morning, hoping that she would wash away the memory of what had happened. She told no one until two weeks later when her aunt eventually got it out of her. By this time she had almost completely stopped eating. She didn't want to go to school and refused to come out of her room. As she related her story, I could see the expression on the faces of her classmates, which reflected a mixture of shock, pity, and admiration for the teenager. So how did her parents deal with us? Anyone who has children could surely relate to the rage felt by her father and the devastation of her mother.

The police were called in, and Sandra was asked to do a medical exam, even though it was two weeks after the incident. However, when the doctor tried to examine Sandra, she had an emotional breakdown. She screamed and fought the doctor, not allowing her to get close to her. Without the medical exam, there was little the police could do except take in the man for questioning. According to Sandra, the police said they had no proof, and eventually he was released and sent back home.

It was now two years later, and Sandra was sitting in my class, trying to live a normal life but haunted by memories that she could not get rid of. I asked if she was able to get some professional help, but she said this didn't work. And what about the guy? Well, at the time Sandra was in my class, incredibly he was still living a few houses down the street from her and even stalked her at times. She was forced to change her phone number. She was never left at home alone, and she hardly ever went outside. I couldn't believe what I was hearing, but I wasn't surprised. The legal system had again failed, something that I was all too familiar with.

Sandra eventually graduated from high school, but her life was a haze of terror, uncertainty, and insecurity. She lived in fear that this man would rape her again, and every day was a struggle to remain sane for her. Sandra's parents eventually enrolled her in the broadcasting school, and she ended up in my class.

It was obvious that Sandra's story moved her classmates as much as it moved me. Many of them had words of advice and encouraged her to be strong and not give up. As they comforted her, I prayed silently, "God, what do I tell this girl? How do I help her?"

After the class I spoke to Sandra at length, and the only thing I could think of was to tell her that God was seeing her pain and that it would soon come to an end. I urged her to take care of herself, to eat, to pray, to put everything in God's hands and not allow another human being to take away her joy.

Sandra told me that day all she wanted was to be at peace. She wanted the memories of that awful day to go away. It didn't help that the animal who raped her lived on the same street as her, and this made her recovery so much more difficult. As I said good-bye to Sandra, I felt such a profound sense of sadness, but I knew that if she believed, everything would be okay.

She walked out of the class that afternoon, and I could tell she was already trying. She held her head high, and her small shoulders were upright, almost as if she was preparing herself to once again face the world.

I didn't have another class with them for the next month, but during that time Sandra called me periodically, sometimes in a panic, and after we spoke, she oftentimes settled down. I felt so helpless. "Comfort her, God. Comfort her," I often prayed.

About a month after Sandra first told us her story, I walked into the classroom, ready for another marathon session. My eyes went around the room, and then I saw Sandra a few rows from the front. *Wait a minute*, I thought. *Is this the same person?* She was all made up. Her hair was done. She was wearing jewelry and a flattering top and trousers. She even looked like she had put on weight. I began the class but looked at her closely. Sandra seemed to have transformed, and everyone in the class noticed it. She was confident. She was actively involved in the discussions, and she even challenged me a couple of times. I was thrilled, but my mind was racing. During the break I pulled her aside and asked her how she was doing. She laughed and told me in a bubbly voice that the most unbelievable thing had happened.

About two weeks before, the guy who raped her was thrown out of his home by his mother. He apparently had nowhere to go and moved into the abandoned house where he had committed that horrible act the day he had raped Sandra. The house belonged to his uncle, so he had permission to live there. A few days later the house caught fire and burned to the ground with all of the man's possessions in it.

Sandra told me that everything she feared had been removed from her life. The man was gone from her neighborhood, and the house that had represented so much pain for her was no longer there. Sandra finally escaped the prison she had been in for two long, agonizing years. I listened to her, close to tears because I knew that God had come to her rescue.

This young woman did what we all need to do when we feel like there is no hope. We hold on, and we ask for God and the universe to help us. She was desperate for help, and God heard her cries. Her story reminds me of something I heard Dr. Wayne Dyer say in one of his meditations, which I have mentioned more than once in this book; however, it is so powerful that I need to reference it again. "If you experience the desperation that causes a man to commit suicide and you feel that you cannot live without seeing God, then you will see God."

Sandra was a living example of this. She was so desperate to see God, and he made himself known to her in the most powerful and beautiful way imaginable. He removed from her life the things that were causing her so much pain. What happened to Sandra has reinforced my own belief in the power that is available to all us to call on and to draw into our lives.

LESSON 13

Nothing Lasts Forever. Your Day Will Come!

I sat in the waterfront restaurant at the Hyatt Regency Hotel in Port of Spain, looking out at the ocean, enjoying my cup of coffee and my oatmeal raisin cookie. Oh, the simple pleasures in life that we so often take for granted. I was supposed to have attended a cocktail reception at 6:30 pm, but I had gotten to the hotel about thirty minutes early. The restaurant faced the Atlantic Ocean, and the view as the sun was setting was breathtakingly beautiful. I observed the waves, the vibrant orange of the setting sun. I smelled the sea and noticed the clouds in the sky, all the while I was thinking, *Why don't I do this more often?* I was thinking about my day, but I decided that I would put it all to rest for the time being and enjoy the moment.

The entire day had been one of interesting experiences, and it seemed like there was a dominant theme throughout. It started in the morning with me attending the opening ceremony of a conference, but then I was asked to move from where I was sitting since that table was reserved. As I relocated, I thought about how I was feeling and why. I felt slighted and even humiliated because my brain processed what had just happened as "you're not good enough to sit at the front of the room." I took a deep swallow, gave myself a hug mentally, and began an inner dialogue that basically focused on some of what I had been reading in that ancient philosophical book, the *Tao Te Ching*. "The lesson here is called the wisdom of obscurity. The gentle outlasts the strong, the obscure outlasts the obvious."

Interesting that I had read this just the day before, and it resonated deeply. For me the biggest takeaway from this thirty-sixth verse of the Tao was that I needed to be comfortable in not being recognized or noticed. My ego, which had always been prominent in my life, needed to be tamed and controlled. The universe, it seemed, had decided to send some very practical lessons in "living in obscurity."

This was no easy task for someone who was once in the spotlight and in front of the cameras. There was a time in my life when I thrived on the recognition I got when I went out in public. I have come to realize that this need to be constantly acknowledged was deep-rooted and went back to when I was a child. There was hardly any positive recognition there. When I was singled out, it was because people wanted to make fun of me, either schoolkids or my relatives. Then as I grew older, this is what fuelled my determination to be in the media.

I thought about this while I had my coffee and cookie. A few minutes later a family entered the restaurant area, and I recognized a familiar face. At first I couldn't figure out where I knew her from. Then I connected the dots. The young lady was the human resources manager at a company I once worked for.

As she walked past me in the restaurant, our eyes met, and I began to smile; however, she walked straight past as if she didn't know me.

I was taken aback but thought, *Oh, well, maybe she doesn't recognize me.* It was soon clear though that she knew exactly who I was. I sat there for about twenty-five minutes, and during that time she would occasionally look in my direction. I was being sent yet another reminder that "living in obscurity" was no easy task, but it was the gateway to peace and self-acceptance.

I paid my check and got up to leave, and as I did, the young lady looked at me again. I'm sure I noticed what appeared to be a smirk on her face.

As I made my way to the event I was supposed to have attended, what came to mind was that "seasons change" and "nothing lasts forever."

A few minutes later I entered the ballroom where the function was just about to start and found a seat in a row almost to the back. One of the persons in front of me turned around, and again it was someone I recognized right away. She, too, worked at the same company, but she ignored me. I went back into that familiar zone of feeling rejected but tried to snap out of it.

During the drive home I meditated and analyzed how I was feeling. As it has happened in the past, that inner voice whispered some much-needed words of comfort. This wasn't an actual voice, but it was more of a thought, a knowing and realization that comforted me immensely. The God inside of me told me, "Every knee will bow, and they will see greatness in your eyes." Yes, I admit this may sound rather egotistical to some people, but for someone who feels rejected and like he or she doesn't matter, there is comfort in knowing that "this too shall pass." It is the proverbial Cinderella analogy. You may be scrubbing floors one day, but who knows what treasures are in store for you.

When you feel like you are not appreciated or even feel humiliated, understand and believe that your day will come! It is important to remain connected to God, your source, and your intentions. What people may try to wrongfully take away from you will be given back to you and multiplied. This may not necessarily mean material things but instead feelings like self-worth, happiness, joy, or accomplishment.

The *Tao Te Ching* advises us that there is a time for everything. Well, my friends, even if "knees don't bow before you," there is so much peace when we "live in obscurity" and let others seek out the attention. I have struggled with accepting this truth for such a long time, and it is still a work in progress; however, I remember the words in Ecclesiastes 3:1 (NKJV), which says, "To every thing there is a season, and a time to every purpose under the heaven."

LESSON 14

It Is So Very Important to Live in Appreciation and Be Grateful

I am grateful for all that I have and all that I have become, for my past, for every experience, every encounter, every person who has come into my life, every disappointment, every setback, and every heartache. I will appreciate my job, my colleagues, my family, and my friends. They are all part of who I am, and every time I am tempted to take this all for granted, I will remember that there really are no certainties in life except that which we cannot see but we must believe in, God, the Creator of universal energy.

Why is it that we so easily forget everything that we have been given and blessed with? It often takes a major shift or incident for us to remember that living in appreciation is one of the keys to internal peace. Like the night when an earthquake measuring 6.2 on the Richter scale shook Trinidad and Tobago and the Caribbean. At around 10:10 p.m. on October 11, 2013, the ground beneath us began to shake violently, and the island went into a state of panic. Thankfully there were no major injuries, but afterward as I observed the reactions of everyone, including myself, I couldn't help but think that this was what it had taken to for us to "wake up and smell the coffee."

Our lives could very easily have been changed forever, and the things that we take for granted could have been snatched away. For those few seconds during the earthquake, as I ran out of my room in a panic and the walls shook, I couldn't even pray because I was so terrified. I knew what it felt like to be completely helpless, and my own humanness became so apparent. I vowed to live in appreciation and to give thanks for all that I had and was.

For many years of my life, I had taken for granted my parents, my job, my health, and the people around me, and I very often wanted more. I was so caught up in the disappointments and the failed relationships, and I was trying to look after my parents, so I forgot to truly, deeply thank the universe and God for life.

One night on my way home from work, I stopped off to get something to eat at a barbeque takeout close to home. It was a roadside family business that was set up in the front yard of someone's home. I parked, jumped out of my car, and stood for a few seconds, looking at the menu, trying to decide what I wanted. I vaguely took note of a man standing to my left and waiting for his order. How this system worked was that you ordered and then paid when you received your order. As I was deciding what I wanted, the man to my left was collecting his. The food smelled delicious, so I opted for the jerk wings and fries.

As I was telling the girl behind the counter what I wanted, the man seemed to change his mind about something, but he very nicely told the person taking the orders to please go ahead and put through mine and that he would wait. He said it in such a nice tone that I couldn't help but look at him and say thank you. A few seconds later he collected his order of chicken and handed the person behind the counter his money. She gave him back his change, and he asked in an almost incredulous tone, "How much was it?

She responded, "Fifteen dollars," which was US $2.50.

The stranger then said to the girl, "Really? That's it? Only fifteen dollars? How much are the fries?"

The girl answered, "Eight dollars," which was US $1.33.

He continued, "Oh, that's good news. Now I can get the box of fries for my daughter. She was begging me to get her some, but we just scraped together the money for the chicken. She'll be very happy to get her fries."

I stood there, stunned. The only thing I could do was look at him and smile. It was his tone that affected me most. This stranger who could barely afford a box of fries was happy and contented with what little he had and felt that luck was on his side tonight since he was now able to buy the box of fries for his daughter. As I processed what had just happened, I repeated silently to myself, "He is happy. This man is happy." I looked at the car he was driving, which was not in very good condition, and I saw the wife sitting in the front seat, the little girl jumping up and down in the backseat.

I was experiencing so many emotions. First there was overwhelming guilt. I felt almost ill when I thought about how much money I spend on clothes, hair, makeup, and food. Then I felt sorry for this family, and I wanted to take care of their bill; however, I thought twice about it since I didn't want to offend the father. All of my issues I was experiencing during the day went out the window because I realized in the scheme of things how very insignificant they were. I thought of my own childhood, which was very much like the one this little girl was probably living. Yes, there were days when my dad couldn't afford to buy me a box of fries, but we were happy like this family seemed to be. They were out together on a Friday night, buying what they could afford. I thought of my own life today, a far cry from my childhood. I thought, *Wow, this family seems to have so little, but they have so much.*

Both the stranger and I collected our orders and walked away in opposite directions. I got into my car and couldn't move. All I could think of was how very blessed I was, and I remembered at that moment to say thank you to God and to the universe. Someone I had never met before crossed paths with me that night to remind me of the importance of being grateful. I most likely would never see this man or his family again, but I will never forget them.

They reminded me that it was oh-so-important to give thanks just like the earthquake had reminded me as well. But I daresay we shouldn't wait for earthquakes or strangers to tell us that life is indeed beautiful and that we should cherish all of it! I no longer question when things don't go how I intended them to because now I understand the dots eventually connect. I know it's difficult to accept disappointments and challenges, but eventually it *will* begin to make sense. When you send out the gratitude energy, things somehow always seem to sort themselves out. It's as if the appreciation and gratitude counters the negative forces. I am so deeply appreciative of everything in my life, including you, the person reading this book. I pray that you will find peace in being grateful and that *Eighteen Lessons* will bring us together as we say to the universe, "Thank you for life."

LESSON 15

The Road May Be Difficult, but St. Francis Did It

As I write this chapter, I cannot help but once again marvel at the awesome power of God. The day had been an interesting one, which brought to the forefront many of the lessons I believe I was meant to have learned during the past few months. I also think that the pathway to the highest level of spirituality is definitely not an easy one. I have fully accepted that living a life of purpose and aligning with God takes courage and determination. At the same time I have come to embrace and welcome the twists and turns in this journey. Recently I have begun to ponder in earnest the story of St. Francis of Assisi, the famous saint who was born in Italy around 1881.

In many ways the story of St. Francis makes me sad, and I often wonder what was going through his mind in his final moments as he lay on his bed with his few remaining friends around him. His life is certainly a testimony of the ultimate sacrifice, but was St. Francis happy during his final days? While his belief in God was unshakeable, did he feel like all of the hardships and betrayals that he endured in his forty-four years were worth it? It pains me to read about his trials even as he remained committed to God and his spiritual purpose. While I would like to embrace spiritually as wholeheartedly as St. Francis did, I don't believe it should have to be filled with such suffering.

I have always known of the existence of St. Francis but never really delved into his teachings until later in my adult life. I also wasn't familiar with his history because I guess he was just someone I associated a beautiful prayer with. But as we have heard numerous times before, "when the student is ready, the teacher will appear." I was reintroduced to St. Francis in earnest when I read Dr. Wayne Dyer's *Wishes Fulfilled* at the end of 2012.

As I write this book, St. Francis has been a source of inspiration and serenity. I can't help but think, *There are so many inspirational books out there, so many people with uplifting and beautiful messages. Will my book have an impact?* Then that inner voice would answer me by saying, "Even if you help but one person, you would be doing what you are supposed to." I remember St. Francis and his unbending devotion to helping others, and I say to myself, "Even if I can achieve a tiny fraction of what he did, then I would have truly lived my life as a spiritual being." I've had this inner dialogue many times, and each time I try to connect with the reason I started off on this journey in the first place. "To serve and help others and to connect as long as I am on this earth with that universal power we believe to be God."

One night while I was browsing YouTube, I came across a documentary based on the life of St. Francis. An hour later I sat in silence in my room with only the sound of the air-conditioning unit disrupting my thoughts. I thought about St. Francis's story, about how he had given up the material trappings of the world to follow a life dedicated to God.

For the first time I gained a full appreciation for the selfless life he led, and it really sunk in that there is indeed immeasurable glory in serving God and humanity. This is what I like to refer to as "soulful glory," the kind that is known to the spirit and God. It is a special knowing that we have deep inside of us and a complete understanding that in everything we do and say, we are connected to the power that gave us life.

So how have I now taken the lessons of St. Francis and applied them to my own life? Well, for starters, I have surrendered to the call that I am here to serve others. In my heart I always knew that this is what I had to do, but I couldn't give up some of those worldly things. I just enjoyed them too much. For many years of my life I have been at a crossroads, not quite sure what I was supposed to do. I have asked repeatedly, "What does it really mean to serve God and others?" In June 2013 I got an e-mail from a woman I had never met before. She asked, "How does one find their purpose in life? I read an article by Wayne Dyer titled 'Living Your Life on Purpose' in which he said we must look beyond whether we should be a doctor or lawyer but move instead to a place of faith in the universal mind. Can you shed some light on this, as I thought purpose, calling, and your gift were all the same?"

My response to her also gave me a sense of clarity.

> Thank you so very much for your message and for your kind words. I am so very happy to know that my writings are making a difference in your life. In fact, I am overjoyed! When I write, I do so with the sole purpose of helping those who read it, so what you have said to me has made my day!

> How is your weekend going? I'm trying to get in as much as possible into these two days. It was so interesting to hear your thoughts on living a life of purpose. In terms of what Dr. Dyer said in his article, I gather that he is alluding to moving beyond a professional title and what society dictates is success. You can be a doctor or a lawyer but not be living a purpose-filled life. My understanding—and this is how I try to live my own life—is to ask the question, "Is what I am doing helping

others in a meaningful way? And most importantly, does it make me feel good?" So for instance, a doctor may be saving lives because of the very nature of the job, but does the doctor himself feel fulfilled? Does the job bring spiritual peace? I believe Dr. Dyer is saying that we need to make the link between what we do and our spirit or the universal mind. Does it make you feel good deep within your soul? If I can use my own life as an example … years ago when I was a journalist and TV news anchor, I was well known. I thought I was helping others, but I wasn't at peace. Even as a communications consultant, I still help people, and to some extent I feel fulfilled. However, my deepest sense of giving back and of helping others comes from my writings and my talks. In trying to discover my purpose in life, I have asked the question, "What makes me feel really good?" The answer is always inspiring others. Hence, I now know what my purpose is in this life.

As for our calling, well, again I will give you my interpretation. When you answer the call, you fulfill your purpose. You can't live a purpose-filled life without first answering that calling. I had to first answer that voice deep within me, that yearning that said to me I was on this earth to inspire others. It was only when I actually succumbed that I began living out my purpose. So the purpose is the end result of answering the call.

You also asked about gifts. Well, we all have gifts, but how we use them determines if we are truly living a purpose-filled life. I have a talent for writing and speaking, which worked for me in media. However, I have now learned to apply these gifts differently. I answered my call, and I'm now using these gifts to fulfill my purpose.

I hope that I have helped you and that things are clearer now. Please let me know what you think. I will certainly look for that article by Dr. Dyer and read it. Have a wonderful weekend!

Blessings,

Ann Marie

St. Francis is still an enigma to me. I am fascinated with his life and with his purpose. What makes a man want to serve God in the way he did? Such unfaltering commitment to fulfilling spiritual dharma, as was the case with Mahatma Gandhi and Mother Teresa. Five years before I wrote *Eighteen Lessons* or even one year ago, I wasn't thinking the way I am today. The spiritual evolution was gradual and is still continuing, and I find it so very helpful to study the lives of these great men and women. Despite the setbacks on my own journey, I will remember St. Francis and use his life as a reminder that there is unquestionable joy and peace in walking a spiritual path. There is serenity in repeating this line from the St. Francis prayer: "Lord, make me an instrument of your peace. Where there is hatred, let me sow love."

LESSON 16

There Is Something Called Unconditional Love

There are some people who come into your life and change everything forever. Well, Antonio is one of them. Ten years after we first met, I still remember the meeting clearly like it was yesterday, and every time I think about that first encounter, I smile. Antonio is my reminder that our souls can reconnect with those whose lives we were part of in another dimension. He is my comfort whenever I doubt my worth because the times spent with him were some of the happiest of my life. It is a deep spiritual love that doesn't need physical contact and will remain strong despite distance or time.

A friend suggested that we may have been brother and sister in another life, and maybe we were. The feelings have evolved over the years from romantic to friendship. There is now that understanding between us that we are connected in spirit. When the thought of someone makes you smile and the sound of his or her voice lights up your world, then you know that the energy is powerful and life-changing. Meeting Antonio was a turning point in my life. He saw an Ann Marie I didn't even know existed. This seemingly unpolished, inexperienced, self-doubting young woman was a cultured and sophisticated princess in his eyes, and he made me feel beautiful inside and out.

Our first encounter was a frightening, powerful, and passionate exchange of spiritual energy, one that at the time I couldn't understand. Today I look back and recognize that it was a soul connection I couldn't identify with at the time. It was carnival time in Trinidad and Tobago, and quite by accident I was introduced to this charming, very handsome, well-groomed Italian businessman. We locked horns several times during that weekend, and I remember clearly that I didn't pass up an opportunity to challenge him during conversations about politics and current affairs. At the time I was a young hotshot reporter, and my brazenness was undeniable. Today when I think of those conversations, I almost want to recoil in horror. Did I really do and say those things? Who was that outspoken person who didn't care about what others thought as long as I was able to voice my opinion? Oh, how times change, and we really do evolve as the years go by. However, that Ann Marie was the person whom Antonio appreciated and believed in.

Eventually our lives went in different directions, and I moved to Florida; however, one incident while I lived there stays with me to this day. I hadn't seen Antonio in years and couldn't even remember the last time we spoke. One night, however, while I was at a restaurant in Miami, I began thinking of him and wondering how his life had turned out. As I smiled to myself, I looked up at the front door, and for a minute I thought I was imagining things. There he was walking through the door in a restaurant in downtown Miami! My jaw dropped, and I sat stunned for a few seconds. It was so surreal. Here I was thinking about him. We hadn't seen or spoken to each other in years. He supposedly lived in Italy, and I had migrated to Florida. What really were the chances of us being in same restaurant at the same time? Not to mention the fact that he had walked through the front door at the exact moment I was thinking about him. I called out to him, and as our eyes locked, it seemed as if time literally stood still. We hugged and laughed as we realized how incredibly amazing it was that we had run into each other.

We parted ways, but I felt at peace and was comforted with the knowledge that our spirits would forever be connected. Antonio taught me about unconditional love, the kind that asks nothing in return and which accepts you for who you are.

Antonio wasn't the only person who taught me about unconditional love. There is Kennedy, I can't even find the words to describe the impact he has had on my life—another soul connection that has to be the stuff that fairy tales are made of. My experience with Kennedy has made it even clearer that we continuously evolve as human beings.

When I met Kennedy, he was about twenty years my senior and living in the London. He was very handsome and accomplished, and he was recognized internationally for his work as an artist. There was something inside that wasn't allowing me to take that step forward, which would have taken our friendship to the next level. Kennedy adored me, and I know he would have treated me with the kindness, respect, and dignity I deserved. I think about those days, and the reality is that at the time I didn't want a calm, levelheaded, and secure older gentleman as my partner. I wanted the adrenaline rush of being with someone younger and daring. Now that I look back at the choices I have made with relationships, I gravitated most of my adult life to these men, "the heartbreakers" as I now call them.

Over the years my friendship with Kennedy blossomed. Then came the day I decided to marry, and this changed everything. We hardly ever communicated during the time I was married, but when I separated and came back to Trinidad, I contacted him. I could sense how heartbroken he was for me because he genuinely felt my pain. In those dark moments when I came back to Trinidad, Kennedy sent me a quote from Marianne Williamson, one that had a huge impact on my life. I felt his love across the miles and the powerful energy from him when I read the quote in my in-box. "Our deepest fear is not that we are inadequate. Our deepest fear is that we are powerful beyond measure. It is our light, not our darkness that most frightens us."

I read and reread this quote numerous times until it sunk it, and I began to accept that I was indeed powerful beyond measure. We all are. It's just that for many of us we just can't see it. Life gets to us and devalues our true worth.

In Christmas of 2012 I felt like there was a shift in his life and that something significant was happening. I contacted him, and as I suspected, Kennedy had found love—a wonderful woman he shared a beautiful relationship with. I was very happy for him, but as I hung up the phone, I felt a sinking feeling in my stomach that I was so very surprised about. I told myself, "I'm doing exactly what I shouldn't do! I'm wanting something only when I can't have it!"

During the next few weeks I couldn't stop thinking about Kennedy, and another phone conversation followed. There was someone I was interested in dating at the time, and I will never forget Kennedy's words. He said, "The only thing I want for you is to know that you are with someone who is crazy about you and loves you as much as I love you."

I finally got it. After all of these years I recognized true love, and it was in front of me all along. The tears streamed down my face silently because I knew that it was too late and that this wonderful, kind human being had moved on and had found his happiness. My prayer for Kennedy was that this woman would be by his side and his partner for life. I knew that he had found his soul mate. I felt such mixed emotions! I cried for the love that I let go, but my tears were also those of happiness that Kennedy had found love. I also cried for myself because I still felt so much hurt, years of pain that could have possibly been avoided. My mantra, however, is this: "No regrets." It all happened as it was supposed to.

Writing this chapter has influenced immensely how I view the people who have come into my life. When I met Kennedy the first time, I wasn't ready. My journey brought me to that place where I eventually was ready, but it was too late. It's like train tracks that change at the exact moment two trains meet at an intersection, but the two trains then go their separate ways in different directions.

I am grateful and blessed to have experienced unconditional spiritual love. What has changed is the lens through which I now view love. It's not always physical and romantic, and even if it is, it can evolve into something much more everlasting. I am fortunate to have had that love from my own parents, and it is one of the greatest treasures of my life. My hope for you is that you are loved unconditionally by a soul that embraces you for who you are and nothing else.

LESSON 17

We Are All Messengers of God

I truly believe that we are all channels through which messages from the divine and the universe could be transmitted. We're like those old-fashioned radios with antennae just waiting to pick up a signal. I certainly never thought when I was younger that one day I would be writing the things I'm writing today. Sometimes I look back at what I've written, and I find it difficult to believe that I actually wrote it!

If I took a closer look at my life, I would say that I don't really think I am uniquely spiritual, which is why I say and truly believe that we all have that ability to change lives and influence the energy field in which we live. We were born with it. Most times we choose to ignore it, or the signs that tell us, "Hey, you have an opportunity. Use it!"

We very often only use it when we are faced with challenges and circumstances that test our faith. It tends to happen when you're at that place where you wonder about the very existence of God as has happened to me in the past. There were times when I was so angry with God that I even wanted to throw my Bible out the window.

During my entire adult life I believed that "bad things don't happen to good people." I thought I was good, so why were these things happening? Every time it did, I thought that God was being unfair. Now it all makes so much sense. Those incidents weren't bad at all. They were my blessings wrapped up in life paper. I eventually got to that stage where I stopped questioning and just lived in a state of expectation and awareness that everything was part of a master plan. We either recognize this is how it works, or we go through life in denial and hating the world when we are faced with the challenges. We often need to get to this stage of absolute desperation before we recognize our connection to our source and the vast energy that is available to us. It is an energy that will allow us to change lives and to set in motion a legacy of goodness and faith in God.

One night in April 2013 as I was driving home from work, I had an experience that convinced me of what I'm writing, the fact that we are all channels or vessels capable of more than we can ever imagine. For that entire week as soon as I left the office and got into my car, I started crying. I felt so betrayed and hurt by someone I trusted and thought I loved. I had gotten to the stage where the pain seemed almost unbearable, and the only thing I knew to do was to place my trust in God. Every time I felt the hurt, I closed my eyes and envisioned light all around me. I knew and felt God was with me and holding my hand.

It's difficult to explain exactly how I made that spiritual connection, but picture yourself standing in a football field with floodlights shining on you. I felt bathed in the light that I knew was God and universal energy. This particular night when I got into my car, I felt different. For starters, I wasn't crying. I still felt connected to my source, but there were no tears, just a knowing in my heart that everything would be okay. My driver's side car window was down, and I felt the cool night breeze blowing. I inhaled deeply, and for the first time in weeks I felt completely at peace. Suddenly I became aware of thoughts entering my mind. It felt like I was being spoken to but not with actual words. I didn't hear a voice; however, I felt a presence within me, and I just knew that I had to write down the words that were coming to me.

I stopped at some traffic lights and grabbed an envelope from my glove compartment. This is what I wrote down:

> One day you wake up and you realize that the sun is shining. You feel the wind blowing on your face almost like it was the first time. Then nighttime comes, and the stars in the sky seem breathtakingly beautiful. All of nature is beckoning to you. There is one universal message. "We were here before you came into this body. We are here now, and we will be here for eternity. If only you would recognize that you are part of us and we are part of you, only then will you fully understand the magnificence of your soul. You would know that in all things there is a purpose. You would understand that your role is to remain connected to us and to your source, and the only way this can be done is through love."

As I was writing, I felt almost like the pen was moving on its own and the words were flowing effortlessly onto the paper. I didn't read what I had written until I got home, and after I did, I just sat there in my room in silence. This was not typically my writing style, and I knew then that for those few minutes I was a channel through which this message had to get out. I had connected deeply with my source, and this was the result. I know this could not have happened had I not gotten to that place of total acceptance and faith in the divine and in the purpose of my very existence.

This is what I mean when I say that we all have the ability to transmit these messages of hope. We can all say to our friends and family that you are not alone. I'm saying to you and humbly suggesting that you accept and understand that your role here is much larger than you think it is. Ask yourself, "What do I want my legacy to be?" If it is that you recognize yourself as a box full of love, as I try to think of myself, then you will no doubt want to share your gifts with others. I am now completely open to divine messages from God and from my source. I live with the understanding that we all have the ability to connect. The key is recognizing it and aligning with the divine mechanisms that make it possible.

LESSON 18

Don't Ever Give Up!

Writing this book has been a great lesson for me in commitment and determination. There were many days when I wondered, *Will it ever get done?* I also questioned myself repeatedly, "Do I have the money to get this book out there? Do I have the ability to write a book?" And oftentimes I asked, "Where on earth am I going to find the time?" I sometimes wished I could escape to some quiet, secluded cottage somewhere by myself away from the distractions of everyday living. Unfortunately I don't have that luxury.

I was sometimes felt like the universe was being unfair and not helping me get to that place of solitude that I needed in order to write. When I first decided to write *Eighteen Lessons*, I was so fired up and energized. Then as the months went by, life got in the way. I had to constantly reign myself back in and reconnect to my mission and purpose. The best way I know how to describe it is to imagine yourself with a rope tied around your waist. Picture yourself swimming out into the ocean, but someone is on the shore, holding on to that rope. Every time you go too far, he or she pulls you back in so that you won't go out too far. That just about sums up how I've managed to not drift out and lose sight of my goal. The person on the shore is actually me, and I'm pulling myself back to shore.

Oh, the distractions of the world! I almost envy some of those well-known spiritual authors who can escape to the countryside or remote beaches where they can look out at the palm trees and write. I have come to realize that there must have been a time when they were like me, walking on a path with a purpose but having to do so in a chaotic world.

So then what do you do? You go deep within and accept that if the thought entered your head at some point, then a seed has been planted. No matter how silly it may be or how unachievable, if you feel in your heart that you are being drawn to an idea and you can't get it out of your head, then nurture it! When I first thought about writing this book, I had no idea where to start. I just knew that I had a conviction. That seed was planted, and I was determined that it would flourish. The process was at times tumultuous. I changed jobs. I had health issues. My mother had her own health challenges, but I just kept on going. There were days when I was so tired after I got home that I didn't even have the energy to check my e-mail. This was different from other projects I had undertaken previously. I admit that several of them didn't materialize for one reason or the other. In retrospect, the conviction wasn't there, but I held on to this one for dear life and reminded myself daily that every day I was getting closer and closer to my goal.

I also didn't allow myself to panic when it seemed like the end was so far away. When I felt anxiety, I repeated to myself, "Everything will happen when it is supposed to." Even the fact that I was procrastinating was part of the bigger picture. I had given myself a deadline of August 2013 to finish, but that date came and went. There were days I just couldn't even bring myself to sit in front of the computer and write. When I eventually started writing again, the entire focus had changed, and I loved the new energy. Even the delays were tied to a bigger picture!

I also did everything I could to imagine the end result, and a major part of this was visualization. I posted the book title on my computer desktop. I repeated it daily. I designed my very own PDF book cover, and I thought about how it would feel to hold the book in my hands. Never had I been challenged like this with a goal. Over and over I repeated Lao Tzu's timeless saying, "A journey of a thousand miles begins with a single step."

I know it's difficult sometimes when we start dreaming and want that dream to become reality. I completely understand how discouraged you may get sometimes, but I have also accepted the difference between surrendering and giving up. I refused to give up and be defeated, but I will, however, surrender it all to God and to the universe. I will also not allow myself to drift out to sea, and I urge you to hold onto that vision and not let it out of your sight no matter what happens.

A few years ago I met an enchanting young woman who changed my life. She had no legs and moved around in a wheelchair. She didn't use prosthetic legs because her legs were amputated too close to her torso as a child. She had this amazing way of lifting herself off of the wheelchair and placing herself onto a regular chair. This person was also what is referred to as a "wheelchair dancer" and had won several competitions in Trinidad and abroad. She worked in an office in Port of Spain and had a boyfriend. I remember our conversations when we first met. She would tell me about her hopes of getting married and having a family. It was easy to think, *Yeah, right*, but when I looked into her eyes, I knew that she had what it took to accomplish anything. She was able to love life, and she had that indomitable spirit of never giving up no matter what.

While I was writing *Eighteen Lessons*, I discovered that she got married and had a child. Imagine that! This young woman who suffered an infection when she was a baby and had to have her legs amputated was living this full and rewarding life.

I remembered this special young woman during the writing of this book, and she is part of the reason I refused to give up. So what if I didn't live in the cottage by the sea? It doesn't matter, because I would not allow myself to find excuses for why I should not complete my project. So when you find yourself drifting out to sea, hold on to that rope and pull for dear life because if God put the dream in your heart, then the universe will conspire with you to make it happen!

Epilogue

I've come to the end of my book and almost couldn't believe it when I finally submitted the manuscript to Balboa Press. I now have the utmost respect for authors because it takes an extraordinary amount of determination and focus to write a book. The process has been one of awakening for more than one reason. I revisited parts of my life that I could barely think about before. I confronted my fears. I realized that things I thought had mattered no longer did, and the things that were not important before suddenly meant so much more. I was able to forgive those I thought hurt me, and I've come to terms with feelings of guilt, which I'm finally learning to let go of. There are still remnants of wounds that are yet to heal, but this is merely a reminder of my own evolution.

One night when I was close to completing the manuscript, I was in my room at my desk, and a butterfly suddenly appeared in the air in front of me. I looked up in wonderment because what immediately came to mind was the cover of Dr. Dyer's book *Inspiration*, which has a photo of him smiling at a butterfly perched on his finger.

My butterfly, which was just visiting, flittered about over my head, landed briefly on my shoulder, and then decided that it would anchor itself on the TV. *There must be a meaning to this*, I thought to myself, so I decided to google the symbolic meanings of butterflies. I read with interest that a butterfly is the symbol of the soul. It could also show purity or beauty. It is a symbol of faith, and the meaning I like the best is "new life and transformation."

What a timely and beautiful reinforcement! I was reminded once again of our purpose in life and our connection to God and the universe. Writing *Eighteen Lessons from Wayne* was indeed a turning point in my life. Every incident was meant to happen so that I could get to this stage. There really are no coincidences and accidents. I choose to take these lessons with me as I continue along my life's journey, and I share them with you lovingly. I have no idea what the future holds, but I know in my heart that whatever happens, I am not alone. I wish you eternal peace and everlasting love.

Namaste,

Ann Marie

CPSIA information can be obtained
at www.ICGtesting.com
Printed in the USA
LVHW100354040422
715238LV00004B/137